Drive and Stroll

Bedfordshire &
Buckinghamshire

Nick Corble

COUNTRYSIDE BOOKS
NEWBURY BERKSHIRE

First published 2006
© Nick Corble 2006

COUNTRYSIDE BOOKS
3 Catherine Road
Newbury, Berkshire

To view our complete range of books
please visit us at
www.countrysidebooks.co.uk

ISBN 1 85306 974 4
EAN 978 1 85306 974 1

Cover picture of Fingest supplied by Bill Meadows

Designed by Peter Davies, Nautilus Design
Typeset by Mac Style, Nafferton, E. Yorkshire
Produced through MRM Associates Ltd., Reading
Printed by Woolnough Bookbinding Ltd., Irthlingborough

Contents

AREA MAP SHOWING THE LOCATIONS OF THE WALKS

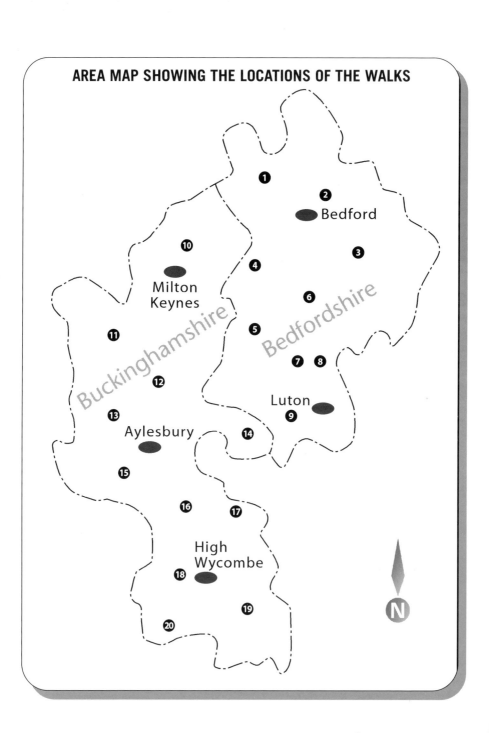

Contents

PUBLISHER'S NOTE

We hope that you obtain considerable enjoyment from this book; great care has been taken in its preparation. Although at the time of publication all routes followed public rights of way or permitted paths, diversion orders can be made and permissions withdrawn.

We cannot, of course, be held responsible for such diversion orders and any inaccuracies in the text which result from these or any other changes to the routes nor any damage which might result from walkers trespassing on private property. We are anxious, though, that all details covering the walks are kept up to date and would therefore welcome information from readers which would be relevant to future editions.

The simple sketch maps that accompany the walks in this book are based on notes made by the author whilst checking out the routes on the ground. They are designed to show you how to reach the start, to point out the main features of the overall circuit and they contain a progression of numbers that relate to the paragraphs of the text.

However, for the benefit of a proper map, we do recommend that you purchase the relevant Ordnance Survey sheet covering your walk. The Ordnance Survey maps are widely available, especially through booksellers and local newsagents.

Introduction

It doesn't matter how long you've lived in an area, there's always something new to discover: a serendipity, a landmark often passed but never investigated, or a historical curiosity unravelled. That's certainly been my experience in researching this book. What's often needed is an excuse to unearth these discoveries and what could be better than combining a drive with a stroll, taking in the chance to sample a local eating place along the way?

Although neighbours, Bedfordshire and Buckinghamshire labour under quite different stereotypes – stereotypes that the walks in this book challenge. Known for its flat prairies, Bedfordshire offers so much more. Sharpenhoe Clappers and Dunstable Downs in the south of the county stand out, quite literally, whilst the densely packed woods of Marston Thrift and Stockgrove are often missed gems.

Buckinghamshire, on the other hand, is rightly known for its beech woodlands, and these feature in some of the walks, but again there is much more to discover. From the Iron Age hillfort of Ivinghoe, which marks one end of the ancient Ridgeway, it's possible to enjoy not only the expanse of the Vale of Aylesbury but also much of the southern part of Bedfordshire. To the north there's a profusion of open water meadows offering a marked contrast to the more forested south.

The two counties also have much in common, notably a pride in the village 'local'. Although not all the suggested refreshment stops in this book are pubs, the quality on offer has often been too good to ignore. Elsewhere, suggestions include a café in England's oldest walled garden and others based in the featured places to visit, where home-made cakes are often a speciality.

The walks are all circular and range from $2^1/_2$ miles to 6 miles in length. Simple sketch maps are included for each route and I have also given an idea of the terrain that will be encountered. The grid references of the starting points are provided as well as the sheet numbers of the relevant Landranger and Explorer OS maps. Don't forget to check the weather forecast before you go and be prepared for the occasional muddy patch – boots or stout shoes are always advisable.

Finally, thanks to all those who have helped in the writing of this book, most especially my family. I hope you will enjoy making the discoveries set out in this pages as much as I did, as well as others of your own. Lace up and happy strolling!

Nick Corble

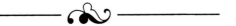

1 | Harrold-Odell Country Park

The historic Harrold Bridge

The Walk: $4^1/_4$ miles
Terrain: A flat and easy start, with a later gentle climb by the side of fields to take in local views
Map: OS Landranger 153 or Explorer 208 (W) GR 956566

How to get there
The Harrold-Odell Country Park is 3 miles north of Turvey, which is on the A428 north-west of Bedford. **Parking:** In the visitor centre car park.

Drive and Stroll

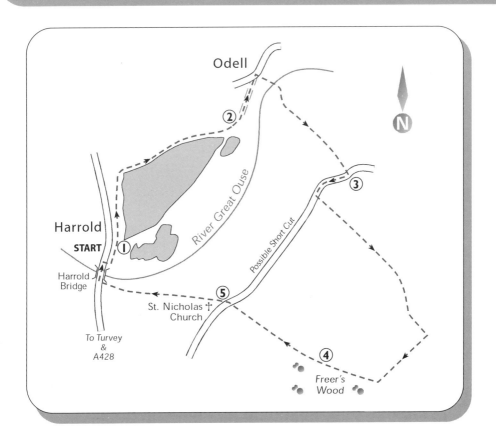

Introduction

This walk packs a lot into a small space. Starting by a large lake that acts as a magnet for wild and birdlife, it goes on to cross the River Great Ouse twice. The first crossing provides an opportunity to see Odell Mill, complete with its old waterwheel, and to spot where the river was diverted to work the wheel, while the second is over the historic and somewhat unusual Harrold Bridge. In between these two crossings, the route climbs up the side of some fields to provide a superb view taking in the whole scene.

The start and finish point is the Harrold-Odell Country Park, where there is a visitor centre with an interesting information and display room. Look out also for the blackboard, which lists recent comings and goings of wildlife visitors to the park. Paths at the start of the walk are solid, although those across the fields can get muddy at times and there's an option to cut this section off and follow a road if you don't feel up to the climb.

The Bell

This pub in Odell (telephone: 01234 720254) is low-beamed, with a number of separate eating areas serving both traditional fare and specials, such as pork and leek sausages in red wine gravy and roasted vegetable pasta fromaggio. Refreshment is also available at the **Café in the Park** (telephone: 01234 720002) in the visitor centre, which serves a varied selection of hot and cold snacks such as beef and ale pie, and some marvellous home-made cakes.

THE WALK

 ①

From the car park, pick up the **red route** round the back of the **visitor centre**, passing through trees. There's an interesting collection of wooden sculptures here lining the side of the path, carved out of old tree stumps. The lake is hidden from view at first although every now and then the vista opens up from clearings. The trees soon thin out and the path bends to the right, following the curvature of the lake. On reaching a T-junction of paths, with a bridleway in front of you, turn left, away from the lake.

Opposite the junction there are some reed beds, which provide a fertile habitat for the common reed and bulrush and wildlife such as reed buntings, marsh harriers, herons, coots and bitterns, all of which are best glimpsed in the summer months.

 ②

Follow the path until it merges into a side road. Keep going past a pair of thatched cottages until you reach the **Bell** in **Odell**. Bear right past the pub down **Mill Lane**, following signs for the public bridleway to **Odell Mill**. The footpath takes you left over the **Great Ouse** via a small bridge above a gentle weir. After this the route is determinedly straight, passing a plantation and climbing steadily uphill until it comes out onto a road.

 ③

Turn right here and stay with the road as it curves first right then left and pick up the footpath on the left just after **Woodside House**. *(Alternatively, take the short cut down the road to point 5.)* The gentle but steady climb resumes, with the path bending slowly right. Be sure to take time here to turn around and enjoy the view. The path turns left and then right to accommodate the corner of a field and then begins to fall. Upon

The old waterwheel at Odell Mill

entering some trees the path bears right before following the left-hand edge of a field and heading right in the corner, passing down the side of **Freer's Wood**, with an abandoned building on your right.

After the wood, cross over a stile and continue heading north-west over some open land. Cross over another stile into a field and stick to the left-hand boundary. It should be just possible to pick out the country park's lake from here. A steady descent follows, ending with a road reached via a metal gate and a stile.

The distinctive spire of **St Nicholas's church** now appears on the left and provides your next target.

The church is, in fact, a youth development facility called the Chellington Centre, and has recently undergone a £1 million investment, which explains the modern antechamber built to take full advantage of the surrounding view.

Cross straight over the road and pick up the footpath, heading down the side of the field with the wire fence to your left. Continue downhill, heading for the gate in the corner. The path now heads out half right, aiming right for a road across an open field. On reaching the road, cross over the stile and turn right, passing over the historic **Harrold Bridge**. The entrance to the country park and the visitor centre is a mere 50 yards on the right, on the other side of the bridge.

Harrold Bridge is first mentioned in 1278 and is notable for the variation in style between its different arches. This is explained by the fact that the bridge sits on the edge of four parishes and the lord of the manor of each parish was responsible for the upkeep of one section. The bridge was restored in 1992.

Place of Interest Nearby

If seeing the Odell watermill has roused your curiosity you may be interested in visiting **Bromham Mill and Gallery** (telephone: 01234 824330) just west of Bedford, where you can see a restored watermill in working condition. Regular baking demonstrations are held and the mill's own stoneground flour is sold.

2 | Wilden

The Victoria Arms at Wilden

The Walk: 3¼ miles
Terrain: Largely flat and easy going, following field edges and some roads
Map: OS Landranger 153 or Explorer 208 (W) GR 095552

How to get there

Wilden lies 2 miles north-west of Great Barford, off the A421, north-east of Bedford. **Parking:** At the Victoria Arms pub for patrons, but please seek the landlord's permission before leaving your car whilst you walk. Alternatively, there is some parking available opposite the pub.

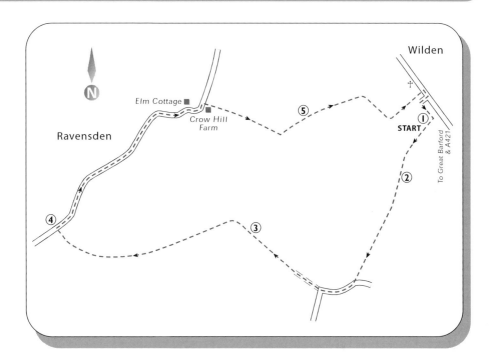

Introduction

This stroll links the two villages of Ravensden and Wilden, with pubs available in each for the thirsty walker, making this a particularly attractive walk on a hot summer's day. Although close geographically, these communities retain their own identity, with Ravensden, in particular, showing a strong individual streak and until recently having its own local dialect.

As the going is easy, mainly across flat and open fields following ancient paths, this is a good route for those who prefer to avoid, or are less able to manage, a gradient. The landscape is dotted with a number of small farms, and it's interesting to note how each has chosen to use their land, with some having established small tree nurseries whilst others prefer to grow more traditional crops. At the journey's end there's Wilden church, an impressive edifice, which can be visited by obtaining the key from the local churchwarden.

Drive and Stroll

The Victoria Arms

This pub in the centre of Wilden is cosy and unpretentious, with a friendly public bar. Memorabilia from the local Bedford Rugby Club is mounted on the walls, along with a jockey's silks, and sits alongside a collection of pub sporting trophies. There's a separate dining area, with the menu offering delights such as butterfly chicken breast cooked Cajun-style and home-made lasagne. Telephone: 01234 772146. **The Horse and Jockey,** near the church in Ravensden makes a good halfway stop. Telephone: 01234 772319.

THE WALK

Starting from the pub, turn right and then right again down **Church Walk,** just before the school, and pick up a footpath on the left just after the school entrance. This skirts a garden and emerges onto a field where you bear right, aiming for a yellow-tipped stake in the corner. Pass through the hedge by the stake and bear to the right. On meeting a junction of paths, head left, following the left-hand boundary of another field.

At the top of the field bear right and then left through a gap in the hedge, resuming your previous southerly direction and heading for a farm. The farm sits on the other side of the road and, when you reach it, turn right and follow the road for 100 yards until it bends sharply to the left. Continue straight on here, down **Avenue Farm Lane**. Pass down the concrete road

leading to the farm through a short avenue of trees.

On the way to Avenue Farm Lane you pass one of Bedfordshire's newest tourist attractions, its Butterfly Park (see 'Places of Interest Nearby' below). An all-weather attraction, it offers the opportunity to view not only tropical butterflies but also to examine a quintessential English landscape.

Stay with the road past **Trent Farm**, coming out into flat fields. Walk on the right-hand edge of these, passing through a pair of metal gates, and on reaching a third, where there's a junction of paths, bear left, with a hedgerow on your right. About halfway down, pass over a plank bridge taking you through the hedge and turn left, maintaining your direction. Pass over a small boardwalk in the corner of the field and keep your south-westerly direction, heading for some houses across the middle of a field. The path bears half right at the end of the hedge and then down the side of a school playing field with metal green gates at either end. This brings you into **Ravensden**.

Until relatively recent times Ravensden had a distinct local dialect all of its own, which included words such as 'umerking' (romping), 'tickere' (get out of the way), 'omperlodging' (arguing) and 'clarring' (in a hurry), a selection which suggests a fairly grumpy community. Ravensden itself was known as 'Ramesden'.

 ④

On reaching a road turn right and keep with it (crossing over to stay with the pavement) as it turns to the right. The pavement runs out and the road twists and turns, eventually coming to **Elm Cottages** by a small pond. On reaching a second pond follow the sign for a public bridleway to the right by **Crow Hill House**. This is partially obscured by a hedge but does exist! On reaching the wooden gate, where the drive turns to the right, head left – although again this is not well marked.

Be careful along here as the road between Ravensden and Wilden is said to be haunted by a strange figure dressed in black, described as a witch with a malevolent character. Don't think you're safe in daylight, as she isn't choosy which time of day she appears!

 ⑤

Follow the next field down its left-hand edge until a sign sends you left over a stile and down a track, with the spire of **Wilden church** peeking out ahead. On reaching another stake pass down the steps and over a boardwalk, bearing right and then over a stile, after which you head left. On reaching a stile before a metal kissing gate, turn left at a junction of paths and pass down the edge of a pasture. This leads out onto the back of the churchyard. Pick up the path through the graveyard and turn right, passing a thatched Tudor cottage. Follow this drive, which bears left back onto the main road and your starting point.

Place of Interest Nearby

Bedford Butterfly Park lies on the route of this walk and is set in a wildflower hay meadow. There's also a tropical greenhouse, which includes waterfalls and verdant foliage where the butterflies fly around you. As if this wasn't enough, there's also a tearoom, gift shop, adventure playground and nature trails. Telephone: 01234 772770.

3 Biggleswade Common

The River Ivel

The Walk: 4^1/$_2$ miles
Terrain: Very flat along bridleways and across common grazing land
Map: OS Landranger 153 or Explorer 208 (E) GR 187453

How to get there

Approaching from the A1 to the south-east of Bedford, turn off eastwards towards Biggleswade on the A6001. **Parking:** In the Dan Albone Memorial Car Park, on the left after the superstore (small fee payable).

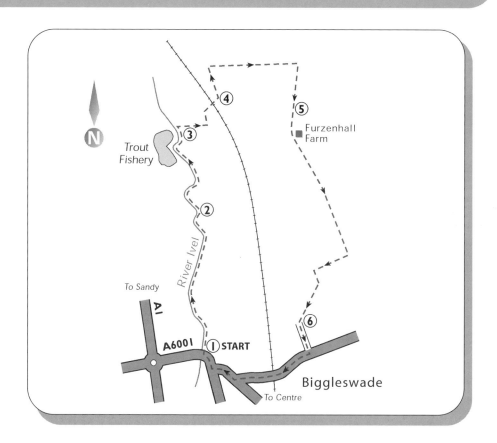

Introduction

This easy walk provides an interesting contrast between the ancient history associated with Biggleswade Common and the various infringements that have threatened it in more modern times, including the railway and a rash of post-war housing. It's still easy to appreciate the splendour of the common itself though, and it's entirely likely that somewhere along this route you will spot some of the wildlife living here, be it a hare, a skylark, a heron or a kingfisher.

The circuit begins with a winding stroll alongside the gentle River Ivel before branching out by a large lake used as a trout fishery. It goes on across the common and under the railway that now bisects it before passing by the farm that sits bang in the middle of the open land. The going is flat and solid and the route ends by taking in the northern lip of Biggleswade, where there is an option to head into the more interesting centre.

The Gardeners Arms

This pub in Potton Road, towards the end of the walk, is a good honest modern hostelry serving the surrounding housing. There's a friendly welcome and plenty of seating inside and out. Food (not served on Monday) is simple but nourishing and includes jacket potatoes, baguettes, fish and chips and an inviting 'combi', including garlic bread, onion rings, chicken wings and goujons. Telephone: 01761 315126.

THE WALK

Start the walk from the **Dan Albone Memorial Car Park**, picking up the path heading right towards the large ironstone fragment by a gate. Pass through a pair of kissing gates and out into open countryside. The **River Ivel** is to your left and is your companion for the first mile or so of the walk.

The car park is named after Biggleswarth's most famous son, an inventor of bicycles, cars and agricultural equipment, including the 'Ivel', the first practical farm tractor, an achievement that gives him a claim to be the father of the British tractor industry.

Stick with the river as it meanders along its course, ignoring the paths to your right, following the top of a raised embankment. Continue over a short boardwalk and past some recently planted trees. On emerging from a kissing gate, stay with the river, keeping an eye out for kingfishers, with this route following another known as **Kingfisher Way** at this point.

Biggleswade Common dates back to 1200. There are 108 Common Rights to the common, gathered together in a representative body known as the Fen Reeves. It is still a working area grazed by beef cattle and horses.

On reaching the lake and cut lawns on the other bank that mark the **Manor Farm Trout Fishery** bear right, keeping the barbed wire fence to your left. On reaching a seat turn right out over the common, aiming for a bridge across a small stream, which you need to pass over. Turn left after the bridge, heading for the cattle arch under the railway, bracing yourself for the possibility of an unexpected Inter City train blasting your eardrums!

In 1850 the East Coast main line railway was constructed over the common and after protests from the Common Rights owners a cattle

The large ironstone passed en route

arch was constructed to maintain
continual grazing.

 ④

Follow the path to the left under the
arch and after passing through
another gate bear left, walking
alongside the railway for a short while.
The path soon diverges to the right
through a hedgerow and meets a
fresh stream, where you bear right,
following the course of the water for
about $1/3$ mile. This marks the
northern edge of the common. After
negotiating a kissing gate and a bridge
turn right, following a bridleway.

 ⑤

Aim for **Furzenhall Farm** and pass to
the right of the buildings when you
get there, through a couple of gates.
The path you are on is known as the
Skylark Ride. You are now walking
out across open land, giving you a
good perspective of the common.
About two-thirds of the way down
this long, straight path pick up the
footpath on the right and on reaching
Furzenhall Road turn left, keeping
with it as it bears towards the right.

*Biggleswade lies at the heart of the
market gardening area of*

Drive and Stroll

Bedfordshire and acts as a market town for surrounding villages. It has its own market square and an Old Market House, and the centre is well worth a visit. The River Ivel has acted as a constraint on development to the west.

Stay with the road as it passes through some houses and at the junction with a more major road turn right. Pass the **Gardeners Arms** and go up over the railway this time, along **Potton Road**, which becomes **St John's Street** after crossing the railway. On reaching another junction turn right into **Sun Street** and finally, on reaching another junction, head right again into **Shoremead Road**, where you quickly come back to the car park.

Place of Interest Nearby

Sandy Warren, just to the north of Biggleswade, is home to the Royal Society for the Protection of Birds. The area has a visitors' car park and a series of trails and hides for spotting – or 'twitching' – birds in amongst its 100 acres of woodland and formal gardens. Telephone: 01767 680551.

4 Cranfield

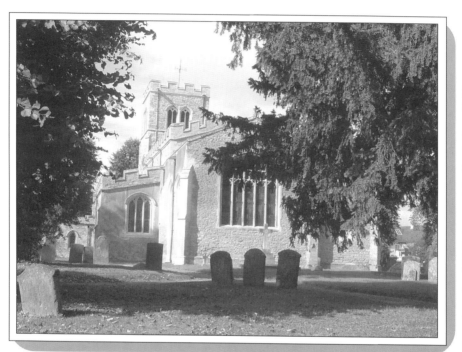

The church of St Peter and St Paul, Cranfield

The Walk: 4 miles
Terrain: A gentle stroll using well-made paths and cycleways as well as some roadside walking. There are two short climbs. The going is easy, although being sited in the edge of a clay ridge some of the paths can get boggy in winter.
Map: OS Landranger 153 or Explorer 208 (W) GR 955420

How to get there
Cranfield lies 2 miles to the west of the A421 between junction 13 of the M1 and Bedford. **Parking:** By the church in Cranfield.

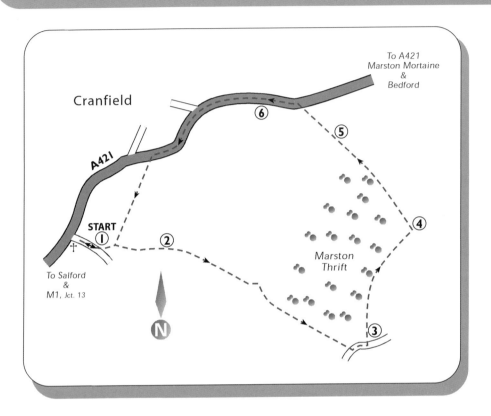

To A421
Marston Mortaine
&
Bedford

Cranfield

A421

6

5

4

START
(1)

(2)

Marston
Thrift

3

To Salford
&
M1, Jct. 13

N

Introduction

Nestled on the side of Bedford is the ancient woodland of Marston Thrift in all its splendid glory. This route has been designed to allow walkers both to experience the brooding majesty of the woods and contrast this with the expansive views round about. For those who want to wander through the heart of the Thrift itself, though, there is a marked path as well.

This walk is particularly suited to late summer/early autumn as it affords some wonderful opportunities for gathering hedgerow fruits, including blackberries and sloes, whilst other berries attract plenty of birdlife in addition to providing a splash of colour.

The Swan

This pub near the starting point of the walk has a traditional bar area, juxtaposed by a very light and modern, wood-dominated bistro area specialising in Italian dishes. Particular delights include the piccante, a dish of spicy Napoli sausage and green chillis, and a long list of pizza choices. Don't miss the strawberry crush for dessert. There's no pretension here, though, and the pub is known as being family friendly and has its own play area and garden. Telephone: 01234 750332.

THE WALK

Start down the road, leaving the church behind you, before heading down **Rectory Lane** on your left after around 100 yards. The path swings to the right and becomes a bridleway, before heading out over open countryside. At a junction of bridleways take the option to the right down a concrete road. This now heads downhill with distant views opening out in front of you.

Stick with the path as it evolves into a cycleway, following the blue arrows signed to **Marston Thrift**. The path now zig-zags its way through recently planted trees until it reaches the south-western corner of the Thrift itself. On reaching another junction of paths head left, following the signs for **Marston Moretaine**. After a while you reach a notice-board after which you need to take the path to the left, following a road for a short while.

Woodland was recorded in this area in the Domesday Book and at that time was probably much greater in extent. Over the following 250 years it was steadily cleared but after that time became more managed, with coppicing used to provide a constant supply of both fuel and building material.

After the second of two houses pick up the footpath to the left and then go left again, heading into the woods briefly by a yellow-tipped stake. You soon emerge onto the eastern edge of the Thrift and you need to walk up alongside this boundary, bearing left to do so, passing a good blackberrying spot. Pass by a defunct stile and then go through two metal gates.

The blackthorn thickets and the replanted elms along this stretch are havens for butterflies in the summer. Elsewhere you may notice shrubs on the edge of the woodland, another deliberate feature designed to provide a favourable habitat for insects.

The Swan inn near the start of the walk

 ④

After crossing over another stile, past the edge of a small tree nursery, the path diverts to the left over a plank bridge. On crossing over the bridge maintain your direction, heading out over a field towards another yellow-tipped stake in the far distance. The views behind you from here are quite spectacular and include the smoking stacks of the **Bedford brickworks**. Follow the path round the side of the woods, keeping the edge to your left.

 ⑤

The first of two short climbs now follows and, on reaching a choice of paths, take the one in front of you over a stile, now heading downhill into a dip before rising again into the second climb. Head for the bottom left-hand corner of the first field where a stile takes you over a bridge and then over a stream. Keep to the left of the hedgerow between two fields as you begin your ascent.

On reaching a road turn left into **Cranfield**. Pick up the pavement and stick with the road as it curves round to the left past the appropriately-named **Thrift View**. Just after **Bowling Green Road** pick up the bridleway signposted to **Cranfield Holywells** to your left. This well-defined track takes you down past the back of some houses and a school playing field. Stay with the main path until you emerge near the junction at the start of the walk where you bear right and retrace your steps back to your car.

The Holywell Spring is ferruginous, that is, heavy with iron, and in the 19th century was revered as medicinal for those with sore eyes. In 1840 this path was designated as a driftway for driving and penning sheep between the dates of 1st April and 14th July.

Place of Interest Nearby

On the north-eastern edge of nearby Marston Moretaine lies the **Forest of Marston Vale Visitor Centre** which, as well as having an exhibition on the wildlife and history of the area, has an art gallery, an adventure play area for children and a café. There is also a number of walking and cycle trails here. Telephone: 01234 767037.

5 | Stockgrove Country Park

The village of Heath and Reach visited on the walk

The Walk: $3^3/_4$ miles
Terrain: Well-defined paths through woods, with some road walking
Map: OS Landranger 165 or Explorer 192 (E) GR 920294

How to get there

The entrance to Stockgrove Country Park is less than 1 mile north of Heath and Reach, which in turn lies just under 2 miles north of Leighton Buzzard via the A4146. **Parking:** There is a car park (small charge) by the visitor centre.

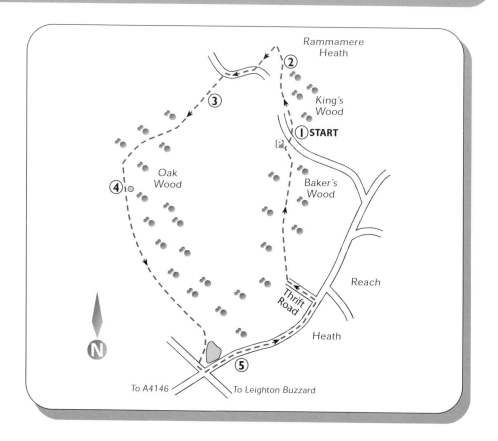

Introduction

This walk offers a pleasant stretch through woodland and managed heathland, along firm and easy paths, and bridleways and a small section of road. The focus of the circuit is Stockgrove Country Park, which was opened to the public in 1972 and covers 80 acres, with a mix of woods, meadows and heaths, as well as a variety of wildflowers. This is a special spot, with heathland of the variety offered here an increasingly rare sight due to intensive cultivation.

If you're here in the spring you will see wood anemones and primroses, and there's usually a profusion of bluebells amongst the trees around May. Look out also for nightjars and tree pipits. The more nervous may also wish to know that adders are rumoured to feature also, although you have to look hard to spot them. There are one or two hills, but nothing too strenuous, and this route should appeal to young and old alike.

Grovers Café

This café by the car park at the visitor centre offers a range of Fairtrade coffees, soft drinks and snacks, including cakes, sandwiches and salads. All profits from the café are reinvested in the management of the park. There's also a family area (where there's a wooden ophthalmosaurus) and picnic site. If you're looking for something stronger to drink, try the **Cock Inn** in the village, telephone: 01525 237390.

THE WALK

Go back to the main entrance to the park and cross the road, picking up the footpath to the left, signposted **'Bedfordshire Circular Walk'**. Almost immediately you pass **King's Wood**, a Site of Special Scientific Interest. Maintain your direction at the end of the fence, going over open ground and through a wooden kissing gate.

King's Wood is so called because it belonged to the king as part of the royal manor of Leighton before 1164. Medieval woodbanks act as borders between woodland and grazing. It is now managed to encourage wildflowers such as heath speedwell, lady's mantle and the wonderfully named devil's-bit scabious.

You now enter some woodland, which comes out onto the edge of **Rammamere Heath**, marked by a bank of firs. Cross over a small track and pick up the path on the other side, heading left and onto the **Greensand Ridge Walk**. On reaching a small parking spot, follow the road to the right, up a slight incline, until the road curves to the right. Pick up the **Greensand Ridge Walk** again by passing through the gates to the right of **North Lodge**.

Continue down the road, taking care to note the tall brick structure in the farm to your left. Although now converted into housing, this was once the water tower for the surrounding estate. Stick with the path as it enters **Oak Wood**, although oaks are very much the exception these days. Keep going straight ahead on reaching a junction of paths. The path goes downhill where there is a sign indicating that the route bears left near a bluebell glade, once again signed as the **Bedfordshire Circular Walk**.

Coniferous plantations such as that in Oak Wood were encouraged after the First World War, which exposed Britain's dependence on imported wood. Trees were planted close together to encourage fast and straight growth, although once a canopy was formed the forest floor was deprived of sunlight, making it unsuitable for most wildlife.

Pass a small pond, part of a much larger trout fishery to the west, and pass through another wooden kissing gate. The path now heads uphill along the right-hand edge of the wood, which here is a mix of oak and beech. To the right are some good views over the **Ouzel valley**. Pass through a clearing, bypassing a stile, and stay with your direction until you reach a path to your right. Follow this down to **Bragenham Lane,** where you turn left and soon come across a four-way junction where you head left towards **Heath and Reach,** near the entrance to **Rushmere Park**.

Heath and Reach are effectively one village with its own village pump and church, St Leonard's, which was originally a private chapel belonging

to Heath Manor House and was given to the people of the village in 1705.

Pass **Rushmere Lake** on the left and continue by the side of the road as it climbs steadily uphill until you reach a pavement at **Heath and Reach**. Just before you reach the junction with the main road turn left up **Thrift Road**, past a school and recreation ground. Go through a gate and to the right of the **Royal British Legion Club** and into **Baker's Wood**. At a fork in the path, keep to the right, again climbing steadily uphill, passing through the wood. This eventually brings you back to the car park and your starting point.

Baker's Wood is another Site of Special Scientific Interest and probably dates back over 1,000 years. The trees here show signs of coppicing over that period and more recent management has brought back some of the indigenous plant life.

Place of Interest Nearby

Leighton Buzzard Railway to the north of the town is a narrow gauge railway built nearly a century ago to carry sand. The track is only 2 ft wide and copes well with the various sharp curves and steep gradients along the 70-minute round trip. Trains run mainly at the weekend from April to October, with a few Christmas specials thrown in. Telephone: 01525 373888.

6 | Flitton: Two Moors

The charming footbridge over the River Flit

The Walk: 3¹/₂ miles
Terrain: Flat across moorland and occasional tracks, with the potential to get marshy on the moors
Map: OS Landranger 153 or Explorer 193 GR 059358

How to get there
Flitton lies just south of the A507 between Flitwick and Clophill. **Parking:** By the church in Flitton.

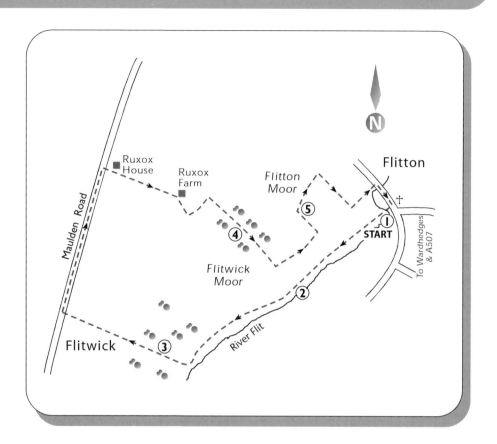

Introduction

This route offers a gentle stroll across moorland and alongside the River Flit and accompanying streams. A particular feature is the opportunity to sample local wildlife and flowers, with each season offering a variation on the walk. The path is well maintained by local volunteers and there are notice-boards dotted along the way giving useful indicators of what to look out for, with kingfishers and snipe a particular feature, so bring your binoculars.

This is also a good opportunity to glimpse an ancient way of life and to learn how the moors once played a vital part in the local economy. Locals rioted when an attempt was made to enclose the area in the 18th century and peat was cut here until recently, both as fuel and latterly as a filter for coal gas. Look out for evidence of railway tracks used to haul the heavy peat. For added interest, there's also the site of a medieval monastic grange along the way.

Drive and Stroll

The Jolly Coopers

This pub at Wardhedges, just east of Flitton, is now the nearest local, the pub in Flitton having recently closed. A traditional low-beamed hostelry with a flagstone floor, open fireplace and an eclectic selection of furniture, with an emphasis on old sewing machine tables, it serves a varied menu from Tuesday to Saturday in its restaurant. Bar snacks and meals vary from feta and onion tart and steak and ale pie through to dishes made with speciality sausages. Telephone: 01525 860626.

THE WALK

Pick up the footpath at the side of **number 3 Church Cottages**. This passes down the back of some houses and comes to a metal kissing gate. Pass through a further gate and over a stream, following the path to the left and alongside the water. Stick with the path and cross over the stream (actually the **River Flit**) by a charming footbridge. Head out over the field and on reaching a T-junction of paths turn left. This is **Maggots Moor**.

Now owned by the Wildlife Trust, this area contains a range of habitats sheltering a number of insects and wildlife now rare in Britain. Designated a Site of Special Scientific Interest in 1954, it is characterised by acidic ironridge waters flowing out from the Lower Greensand aquifer. The area is grazed to encourage the growth of wildflowers, including meadow saxifrage and lady's smock. Also look out for water rail and banded demoiselle damselflies.

Pick up the path on your right marked '**Two Moors Heritage Trail**' through a wooden kissing gate, cross over a small wooden footbridge and walk onto **Flitwick Moor**. Pass through another similar gate and take the right-hand fork heading towards some trees. Go over a wide footbridge and turn immediately left. Follow the path to another bridge, and turn right immediately after it and through a wooden kissing gate into the trees.

A 19th-century portrait of locals cutting peat on the moor painted by Thomas Fisher was recently discovered at a dealers and money was raised to buy it and display it locally.

The path crosses a stream once again and for a short while becomes a boardwalk. Pick up the path on the other side and you soon come

Flitton church at the start of the walk

out onto a track where you turn right and then left, following the track down to the road. On reaching the junction with the main road, cross over and pick up the footpath. Head right along the road, keeping with it as the footpath runs out, for a total of 200 to 300 yards until you reach **Ruxox House** on the right. Cross back over and pick up the public footpath to the right of the house, heading towards **Ruxox Farm**.

There's been a farm here for millennia. The name Ruxox derives from 'hroc's oak', 'hroc' being Saxon for farmer, although some still-visible earthworks are thought to

date back to the Iron Age. In the 12th century this was also the site of a medieval monastic cell for retired monks from Dunstable Priory. The modern complex is a 'model farm' created in the 1850s by the Duke of Bedford's estate.

Follow the path round to the right between two fields and through an avenue of limes, which may or may not be a Roman road. Follow the path as it dog-legs round the right-hand edge of a field, aiming for some trees and a yellow-tipped stake. Continue straight on at the stake, keeping the stream to your right. On reaching a small open area with a seat, bear left and head through a birch wood via a kissing gate.

The path follows three sides of a square, turning right and then right again around an enclosed section of the moor. It then comes out onto a track where you turn left and then immediately right across a concrete bridge over the **Flit** once again. Pass through yet another kissing gate and down the lane to return to your starting point.

Place of Interest Nearby

The **De Grey Mausoleum** adjoining Flitton church dates from the 17th century and houses the funerary monuments of the De Grey family, the earliest of which dates back to 1545. The collection is regarded as of national importance because of the quality of the pieces and the examples they provide of changing tastes, with styles varying from Baroque through to Classical and Gothic. To visit you need to pick up the key (telephone: 01525 860094) and provide advance notice. Visits are possible at weekends only.

7 | Harlington

Harlington village

The Walk: 5 miles
Terrain: Mainly solid, with a few gentle climbs
Map: OS Landranger 166 or Explorer 193 GR 037304

How to get there

Harlington is 1 mile east of the A5120 just north of junction 12 of the M1.
Parking: In the village hall car park, to the south of the main crossroads in Harlington.

Drive and Stroll

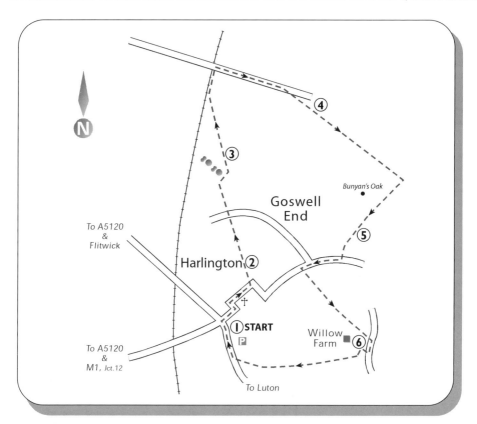

To A5120 & Flitwick

To A5120 & M1, Jct.12

Goswell End

Bunyan's Oak

Harlington ②

Willow Farm ⑥

① START

To Luton

Introduction

This walk follows an undulating route along a combination of bridleways, footpaths and roads. It takes you through some pretty Bedfordshire countryside and in the footsteps of John Bunyan, one of the county's most famous sons. The circuit takes in a chance to see Bunyan's Oak, where Bunyan preached to a small crowd and was arrested for his efforts, being taken to Harlington Manor for interrogation. There are some excellent views along the way, including one of Sharpenhoe Clappers, a promontory that sits proudly above the surrounding flat landscape, and another over towards the north of the county.

Harlington itself is famous for its collection of half-timbered houses, some of which date from the 15th century. The village's history extends much earlier though, with evidence of an Iron Age hillfort taking advantage of the village's lofty position and of a Roman cemetery nearby. The church is also noteworthy and dates from the 13th century.

The Old Sun

This is a pleasant and unassuming half-timbered pub just down from the village hall, with a bricked-in inglenook fireplace and walls clad in black-stained wood. There's a non-smoking eating area as well as a small beer garden with children's play equipment. Food varies from steaks and grills to well-filled baguettes and jackets. Telephone: 01525 872417.

THE WALK

Turn right out of the car park and right again at the crossroads, heading towards the church. Follow the road round and pick up the path on the left, which leads you down an unmade road called **Churchills**.

Sitting in an elegant churchyard, Harlington's church of St Mary the Virgin was originally built by the Augustinian monks of Dunstable Priory. These days the village's associations with John Bunyan are acknowledged with a stained-glass window depicting scenes from 'The Pilgrim's Progress' and an altar made from a bough from the tree Bunyan preached beneath at Upper East End.

The path passes downhill and through an alley to a residential road where you cross straight over and past a school playing field before emerging onto another road, which you follow down to a T-junction. Turn left and pick up the path on the opposite side of the road after about 20 yards. This cuts across fields and heads towards woodland. On reaching the trees the path bears right, sticking with the edge of the field, passing through woods on the left after a short climb.

On emerging from the trees pass straight ahead over an open area, through a hedge, and then over to the right for a short while before picking up the path that runs parallel with the hedge in the same field down towards the railway track. You are now on the **John Bunyan Trail**. After passing through a hedge the path runs parallel with the railway for a short while before meeting a road by a bridge. Turn right and follow the road until you reach a bend and pick up the footpath slightly to the right.

Stick with the track as it crosses open fields, looking out towards a magnificent view of **Sharpenhoe Clappers** (see Walk 8). On reaching a crossroads of paths go through the gap in the hedge on your right

Drive and Stroll

before some new housing. Head downhill towards a corner in the field and the walk's first stile.

The rather lonely looking tree near the centre of the field on your right is Bunyan's Oak. Around 600 years old, the tree is said to have a natural growth that provides the perfect preaching spot. It was for his preaching here that Bunyan was interrogated at Harlington Manor, his actions being thought of as seditious.

Continue to the base of the field, going through a gate, and pass along the edge of the steep hill ahead to the left. On joining another path head right up towards the top. Once again, there are some magnificent views here, looking north. Pass through another stile and then a third, which brings you out onto a road where you turn right. Stay on **Barton Road** on entering **Harlington** for about 20 yards until you pick up a footpath on your left. The path immediately heads rapidly downhill

through mature hedgerows and comes out by an old farmhouse, **Willow Farm**.

Turn right here and pick up the footpath on the right by a double metal gate. On reaching a hedge bear left along the side of a field, with a row of Harlington's houses up on a ridge to your right. At the corner of the field, cross over the hedge and bear right, picking up the path that then bears half left across an open field towards some trees and houses. Head down the alleyway behind the houses and on reaching the road opposite the **Old Sun** bear right and follow the road back to your starting point.

The Old Sun has been a pub for over 200 years and a list of all the landlords since 1785 hangs inside, along with the different names it has gone under. At one point, beer was delivered by steam wagons, but they had to give up when they couldn't cope with the incline of Sundon Hill.

Place of Interest Nearby

Luton Museum and Art Gallery on the north side of Luton has some excellent displays on the local industries of millinery and lace making, as well as a good summary of local history, all housed in an old Victorian house in Wardown Park. Telephone: 01582 546739.

8 Sharpenhoe Clappers

Sharpenhoe Clappers

The Walk: 4 miles
Terrain: Across fields and woodland, with a few steep climbs
Map: OS Landranger 166 or Explorer 193 GR 066296

How to get there

Sharpenhoe itself lies 1 mile west of Barton-le-Clay off the A6. **Parking:** There is designated parking for Sharpenhoe Clappers on the minor road south of the village.

Drive and Stroll

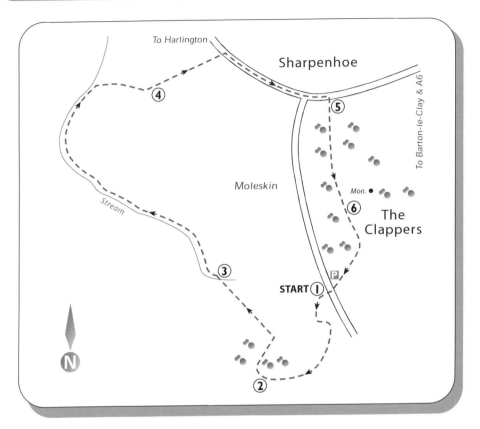

To Harlington

Sharpenhoe

To Barton-le-Clay & A6

④

⑤

Moleskin

Mon. •

⑥

The Clappers

Stream

③

P

START ①

N

②

Introduction

Although at times challenging, Sharpenhoe Clappers positively demands climbing. It stands proud amidst a glacial, and therefore flat, landscape, with a magnificent display of beech trees crowning its top. This circular route has been designed to allow the walker to appreciate the view from afar and from the top. It starts with a stroll along the promontory's southern edge before wandering alongside one of the area's many chalk streams and lining up a final ascent.

There's no doubting Sharpenhoe Clappers' dramatic position, which has attracted not only man but, some believe, aliens also. The surrounding fields see crop circles in the summer and the site is favoured by mystics and lovers of ancient mysteries. The name 'Clappers' derives from the Latin 'claperius' meaning rabbit hole, with local warrens providing a constant supply of protein and skins to the local people in Roman times and beyond. The flora and fauna also include a wide variety of butterflies and wildflowers in the spring and summer.

The Lynmore

This pub in Sharpenhoe, at the junction where the road leads up to the car park, is very popular. It offers an extensive menu and a separate dining room, as well as lounge and public bars, the latter retaining its traditional dartboard. Diners can choose between exotic blackboard dishes such as guinea fowl, with braised cabbage and bacon, or cod in crispy ale batter through to snacks or, should the fancy take them, scrambled eggs with smoked salmon. Telephone: 01582 881233.

THE WALK

Cross over the road from the car park and pick up the footpath directly opposite. Go up some steps and through a metal kissing gate. Strike out half left through another metal kissing gate in the corner of the field. The path heads immediately to the right and then left along a steep slope, with some good views out to the right through the trees. After meeting another path from the left, the walkway widens out a little and continues through the trees and along the edge of the escarpment.

The area at the base of the escarpment is known as Moleskin. It was here that local farmers cleared the wildwood and mined the chalk for lime to put on their fields. These days the fields have their own ecology, with the sunny south-facing slopes providing a magnet for insects and birds.

On reaching a T-junction of paths, take the right-hand option, down some steps through the woods, passing through a wooden kissing gate at the bottom. Continue straight ahead into a field and bear left in the corner along the side of a mature hedge. Cross over a plank bridge and maintain your direction, ignoring the path to your right, keeping to the left of another hedge and following the line of a stream.

After a while cross over the stream and pick up the path to your left, following a rather bumpy chalk track, with a good view of the **Clappers** behind you. Stick with the stream as it bends to the right. Stay with the stream until you meet a crossroads of paths, where you bear right, continuing with the field and leaving the stream behind you. After a short climb uphill, the path passes through a clump of trees and then leads you along the edge of the field.

41

Drive and Stroll

 ④

With the **Clappers** now straight in front of you bear left, heading towards a farm at a three-way junction of fields. On reaching a road bear right into **Sharpenhoe village** and follow the footpath along the main road, past or into (as takes your fancy) the **Lynmore pub**. Just after the layby beyond the crossroads pick up the footpath labelled '**Chiltern Way Extension**' on your right.

This view of the Clappers is said to have influenced John Bunyan, the author of 'The Pilgrim's Progress', providing the inspiration for the book's 'Delectable Mountain'.

 ⑤

Now comes the tricky bit. The steady ascent up the **Clappers** begins. Although the beech trees on the top make it look taller than it is, the hill still represents a good climb, although life is made easier by the provision of some steps. On reaching the top, pause to get your breath and admire the view.

It comes as no surprise to discover that the Clappers proved an early attraction to Iron Age man, with the hill's defensive qualities more than obvious. Imagine it cleared of its beech trees and offering unfettered views north towards Bedford, east to Hitchin and west towards Toddington.

 ⑥

Pass to the right through the trees until you reach a monument, which tells how the site was acquired by the National Trust, with money bequeathed by W.A. Robertson, in memory of his brothers who fell in the Great War. Pass down a dip beyond the monument and pick up the path that runs just to the right of a barbed-wire fence, with trees to the right and a field to the left. This rejoins the **Chiltern Way**, with more steps taking you down and along back to the car park.

Places of Interest Nearby

Barton Hills National Nature Reserve, to the south of Barton-le Clay, off the B655, is a haven for chalkland flowers, insects and butterflies. **Barton Springs**, just up from Church Road in the village was a popular spot for day-trippers at the turn of the 19th century who would come to see the wild watercress that grew in the chalk stream, although today the flow of the stream is much reduced.

9 | Dunstable Downs

The view from the top of the downs

The Walk: 6 miles
Terrain: Generally good paths, with occasional gradients
Map: OS Landranger 166 or Explorer 182 GR 008198

How to get there

Dunstable Downs Countryside Centre is on the B4541 to the south of the junction with the B489, just over a mile north of Whipsnade. **Parking:** In the National Trust car park.

Drive and Stroll

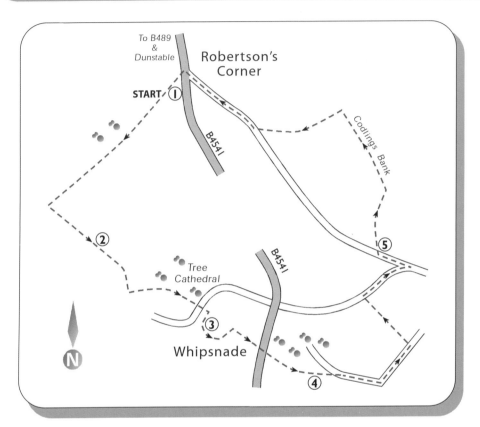

Introduction

This circuit starts with commanding views over Dunstable Downs, including the base of the London Gliding Club whose white planes and transporters lie like shattered shards of white china. In the early stages of the walk you may get very close to the silently swooping gliders! It's worth bringing a map and binoculars and seeing how many landmarks you can pick out.

This route is much more than the Downs, though. It also includes the unusual Whipsnade Tree Cathedral, a living monument in more senses than one as it is still used for public worship today. You will pass through Whipsnade and out over fields, then up along the edge of the Downs on a slope known as Codlings Bank. The views here provide a contrast to those at the start of the circuit but are no less spectacular, especially when the sun casts long shadows. This is not a walk to rush, and indeed some of the gradients involved make it impossible to do so, but it isn't too strenuous and any effort involved is amply rewarded.

The Old Hunters Lodge

This pub, on the southern edge of Whipsnade, is a distinctive building with a half-timbered façade, a thatched roof and a large garden, which is generously filled with ornate furniture. Inside, a low-beamed bar offers meals such as moules marinière, grilled sardines with garlic butter, sautéed garlic tiger prawns and a good vegetarian selection. There's also a separate restaurant. Telephone: 01582 872228. Alternatively, the **Countryside Centre** at the starting point offers a range of basic hot and cold food and drink. Telephone: 01582 608489.

THE WALK

Walk downhill from the car park and pick up the **Icknield Way** by some scrub, heading left. The path soon becomes more defined, passing across open ground via a gate. Go through another gate and just before a car park head up left and then right before passing through a pair of hedges, leaving the views behind you.

Dunstable Downs are owned by Bedfordshire County Council and the area is a startling example of a chalk down, with the land rising up as high as 800 ft above sea level. The Downs are also remarkable for the range of butterflies that thrive here, including the Chiltern gentian, chalkhill blue and Duke of Burgundy.

The path now heads gently downhill. After passing a couple of

houses bear sharp left and over a stile. Follow the right-hand edge of a small pasture and go through another gate on the other side. This leads you into the grounds of the **Whipsnade Tree Cathedral** where it worth lingering a while. On leaving the **Tree Cathedral** pick up the path once again and walk down to a small car park where you bear right.

The Tree Cathedral was founded in 1931 by E.K. Blyth as a place of worship, partly in memory of friends lost in the First World War and partly because he had been inspired by the building of Liverpool Cathedral. It is now owned by the National Trust who maintain the collection of trees, which include ash, beech, cherry, lime and cedar, with a variety of shrubs also present.

Cut across a triangular green and down a small road opposite, which bends to the right by the distinctive **Old Post Office**. Turn left down the metalled road, picking up the footpath on your left, leaving the

Drive and Stroll

Icknield Way. After another kissing gate turn right along a field and on reaching a road turn left, crossing over to head right after around 40 yards, passing down the edge of a wood. Go down an alleyway by some houses and turn left down a footpath after **number 24**.

This heads right through some woods following the line of a road to your left, eventually bearing sharp right. Take the path to your left here, turning right at the road and then left up **Dovehouse Lane**, heading uphill. Pick up the footpath on your left at **Shortgrove Manor Farm**, passing over open ground. On reaching a road head right, initially along the side of the road, although there's soon a path to the left, which curves and joins a residential road where you turn left.

Pick up the footpath on the right at **Maylords Farm**, where it ducks

under a horse chestnut tree and then heads right over a series of stiles, eventually heading downhill through a narrow pasture to the right via another stile. Just after the path starts to rise again, turn left and cut across the following field, along **Codlings Bank**, eventually descending through trees. Stick with the path as it skirts the edge of some woods, heading uphill, and then through the trees by a stable to reach **Isle of Wight Lane.** Turn right and follow the road back to **Robertson's Corner**, marked by a plinth, where your starting point becomes clearly visible once again.

Continuing the theme of remembrance, Robertson's Corner is so called because this piece of land was bought with money bequeathed to the National Trust by W.A. Robertson in memory of his two brothers: Norman, who died in Hanover, and Lawrence, who died in the Battle of the Somme.

Place of Interest Nearby

As well as the Tree Cathedral, Whipsnade is, of course, famous for its **Wild Animal Park**. One of Europe's largest wildlife conservation parks, Whipsnade is part of London Zoo and is home to more than 2,500 animals, including a number of species endangered in the wild. Telephone: 01582 872171.

10 | Newport Pagnell

The 18th-century Dolphin pub in the High Street

The Walk: 3³/₄ miles
Terrain: Flat, through meadows and along some pavements
Map: OS Landranger 152 or Explorer 207 (E) GR 878439

How to get there
Newport Pagnell is just north of Milton Keynes off the A422. **Parking:** In one of the town centre pay and display car parks.

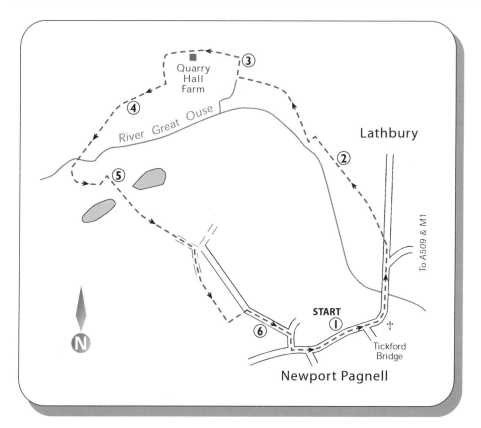

Quarry
Hall
Farm

③

④

River Great Ouse

Lathbury

②

⑤

To A509 & M1

N

START
①

⑥

†

Tickford
Bridge

Newport Pagnell

Introduction

Newport Pagnell has got used to living in the shadow of Milton Keynes, but it has a long history of its own. An Anglo-Saxon town, which became a fortified borough, its high position has led it to be popular with invaders over the centuries, although it owes its living to its position as a market town. The presence of the River Great Ouse to the north has also been significant and this walk provides the opportunity to sample a short section of the river and see how it ties in to the town's history.

Starting off across North Bridge, built in 1810 when the Manchester stagecoach fell off its predecessor into the water, the walk traces a path along a quiet stretch of the river, allows the walker to appreciate a vista of the valley it forms and finally crosses it again by some old gravel pits filled with water. There's only the occasional climb and plenty of opportunities to sample the wildlife alongside the water and in the hedgerows before walking the length of the High Street where there are many historical reminders.

The Dolphin

This inn on the High Street dates from 1740 and is a typical town centre pub with two bars. Good pub grub using organic meat is offered, as well as some unusual dishes such as tomato, red onion and mozzarella pie. Telephone: 01908 611370. Alternatively, you could try one of the many snack bars in the town, among them **Truffles** (telephone: 01908 614132) and **The Coffee Pot** (telephone: 01908 617931).

THE WALK

With the church at your back, head north out of the **High Street** and over two branches of the **River Great Ouse**. Stick by the side of the road and pick up the footpath on your left just after a hedge. This bends half right over a pasture and crosses a minor road before skirting **Lathbury Park**. Stay on the path as it crosses another road and passes between two fences.

Lathbury gets its name from the hazel and willow sticks that grew on the marshes besides the river, which were cut to provide the laths for wattle and daub houses. The church of All Saints is thought to lie on Saxon foundations although the oldest remaining part is the 12th-century nave.

On leaving **Lathbury** the path heads out over meadows, with a short turn to the left, before resuming its previous direction at the end of a field. Here you make your second acquaintance with the **River Great Ouse**. The path bears right along an arm of the river, following the edge of a field with trees to the left.

The river is easily traced by its willows and reeds, and, in summer, look out for the occasional turquoise flash of a dragonfly and a wide variety of butterflies in the hedgerows.

Stay with this as it curves left and then sharply to the right, heading for a line of immature horse chestnuts. Turn left on reaching a road and follow this down to **Quarry Hall Farm**. Pass to the right of the farm buildings and pick up the footpath on the left, which takes you over the farmyard before the final cowshed. Cross a stile and stick with the left-hand edge of the next field, turning right in the one that follows and sticking with the boundary until you reach a disused building. Strike out half left here towards a stile, to the left of a clump of trees marking a disused limestone pit.

The River Great Ouse

 ④

The views here look out over the **Great Ouse Valley** and the river itself. Cross the stile and maintain your direction over the next field to another stile. After this, cross the river using the functional metal bridge on the left and follow the track after it, heading half left. Pass over another stream using a concrete bridge slightly to the left.

 ⑤

Bear left and the path shortly curves to the right, passing between two lakes and up towards some trees. After a gate the path heads further uphill and emerges onto a junction of roads where you fork right. Follow the line of the allotments to your left across **Bury Field** until you reach a children's play area where you pick up the path heading right.

Bury Field is all that remains of common land where locals used to farm strips of their own land, with pasture rights held by the merchant owners of town properties or 'burgages'. Some common-right owners remain to this day.

This brings you out onto a residential road where you head right. Follow this down to the main road where you turn left. Go past the **fire and police stations** and back into the **High Street** and your starting point. Take the opportunity to take the right-hand turn in the town centre to look at **Tickford Bridge**.

Tickford Bridge is a Grade II listed ancient monument built in 1810 to a design by Thomas Wilson. The bridge is an iron masterpiece sitting on two stone abutments and it is this, combined with the fact that all the joints are pegged and are in compression, that gives the structure its remarkable strength.

Place of Interest Nearby

A must see while you're so close to Milton Keynes are the city's famous **concrete cows** (park in the City Discovery Centre car park just off H3 in Monks Way, Bancroft). The cows were constructed in 1978 by community artist Liz Leyh, with the help of local school children, using scrap materials. They have had a colourful history, including once being painted as zebras!

11 Tingewick

The weir at Tingewick Mill

The Walk: 4 miles
Terrain: Mainly fields and farm tracks, with minimal hills
Map: OS Landranger 152 or Explorer 192 (W) GR 655328

How to get there

Tingewick is 2 miles west of Buckingham, just north of the A421. **Parking:** There's on-street and some layby parking in the village.

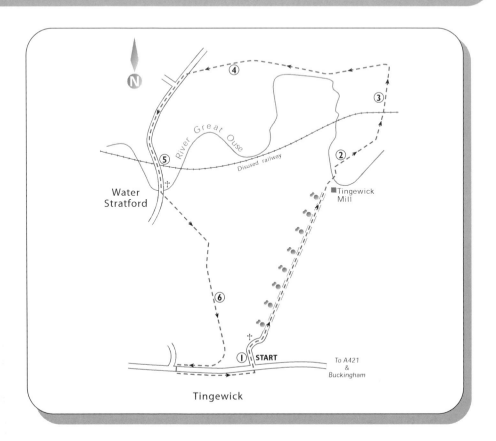

Tingewick

Introduction

Passing through the pleasant water meadows of the River Great Ouse, this walk provides a glimpse of how life once was for the small villages of Tingewick and Water Stratford, taking in an old mill and a disused railway line along the way. Tingewick, in particular, is worth pausing in for a while to absorb a collection of architectural styles, including the Old Sunday School, with its 1828 inscription, and Eagle House, with its statuary of the said bird gazing out onto the Main Street.

The water meadows provide an opportunity for nature spotting and lead to Water Stratford, which these days is a quintessential English shire village guarded over by a church on a slight hill. Walking along this route presents few challenges, so there's plenty of opportunity to enjoy the surrounding countryside.

Drive and Stroll

The Royal Oak

Towards the western end of Tingewick, the award-winning and characterful Royal Oak has two distinct bars, merging together by the front door. There's a beer garden and also a dining area where you can enjoy the pub's specialities of tagliatelle carbonara or lasagne verde, or feast on more traditional favourites such as fish and chips, steaks or ploughman's. Telephone: 01280 848373.

THE WALK

###

Head up **Church Lane**, bearing right on reaching the church and staying on the road as it swings left and becomes a track heading north-east. This follows a straight line for a mile heading for **Tingewick Mill**. A solid path, the route passes between two hedgerows with fields either side. On reaching the mill (look out for the wheel) the path crosses the **Great Ouse** via a metal bridge by a weir. Bear left briefly and enter another field.

Tingewick Mill dates back to the Domesday Book and as late as the 1930s eels caught here were sold at Billingsgate Market.

###

The footpath now cuts across this field, heading out half right along the boundary. About two-thirds of the way down, the path diverts to the left over a stile. There's an easily missed gap through the hedge now in front of you, about 30 yards from the right-hand edge. This should not be confused with a wider opening further to the left. Go up some steps to the top of the embankment that once carried a railway track.

The Buckingham and Brackley Junction Railway that used to run here was completed in 1850. Water Stratford briefly enjoyed its own 'Halt' when it was selected for a 'railcar' experiment, with olive green railcars running between Buckingham and Banbury. The service ceased in the 1960s.

###

Pass back down steps, over a stile and slightly to the right, keeping a wire fence to your left. On reaching a stile turn sharp left and pass along the edge of two fields, meeting the **Great Ouse** towards the end of the second of these. Keep going with the river to your left. After a few hundred yards the water diverts to the south and the path heads uphill past a derelict farm building. Just after this bear left at another stile, over a plank bridge and through a hedge.

The statue of an eagle stands guard in Main Street, Tingewick

The River Great Ouse rises just north of Brackley and empties in The Wash. The river is prone to flooding here resulting in wet meadows, which provide a habitat for species such as ragged robin and cranesbills. Look out also for reed-mace, with its poker-shaped flower.

Keep your direction across the next field, passing over another stile to the left of a metal gate. The path continues to the left of the farm over a series of stiles until you reach a road where you head left down through the pretty village of **Water**

Stratford, with its thatched chocolate-box cottages and manor house.

In 1693 John Mason, the rector of Water Stratford, proclaimed the Second Coming would occur in the village over Whitsun and hundreds descended to witness the event. Sadly he died in the excitement, but the crowds lingered as Mason had proclaimed he would rise again after three days, with many subsequently claiming to have seen him.

Cross back over the railway and river and pick up the footpath on

the left on a bend. This heads half right over a pair of stiles by a section of relatively new wooden fencing. After this, head out even more to the right across the corner of a field where another pair of stiles awaits. The footpath passes to the right of the house in front of you, going down a channel with kissing gates either end. Crossing over the driveway the path maintains its direction over a series of stiles.

After another kissing gate there's a choice of paths where you need to head right. A succession of roped and chained kissing gates follows as the path curves away to the right round the back of some houses. On coming out onto some steps, head down to the road and bear left, then left again back into **Tingewick's main street**.

Place of Interest Nearby

The Old Gaol in nearby Buckingham is an early example of 18th-century Gothic architecture. It houses a museum telling the story of the town, as well as the gaol itself, which was built as part of a failed campaign for Buckingham to regain its status as the county town. Telephone: 01280 823020.

12 Stewkley

The gentle countryside around Stewkley

The Walk: 5 miles
Terrain: Mainly flat along field boundaries, roads and pavements
Map: OS Landranger 165 or Explorer 192 (E) GR 854254

How to get there
Stewkley is just south of the B4032 connecting Winslow and Leighton Buzzard. **Parking:** In the car park of the Carpenters Arms, with the landlord's permission, or alternatively on the road.

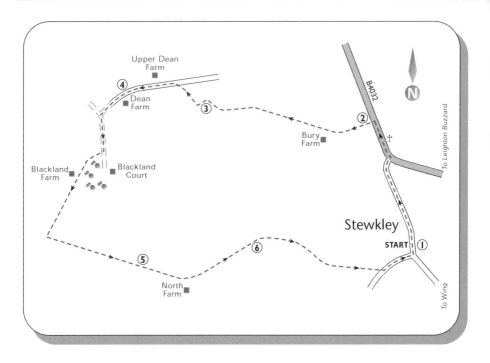

Introduction

Offering a variation on the erratically marked Stewkley Circular Walk, this route has been designed to allow the walker to appreciate how Stewkley earned its title as 'the longest village in Britain', something it's easy to believe as you walk down the High Street. The route passes by and near a number of working farms and evidence of continuing farming activity is a feature of this circuit.

This is an easy walk, with plenty of variation. As well as woodland in the form of Blackland Covert, there are some quite magnificent views. There are also a number of ponds along the way, including one quite near the start, which would make an ideal picnic spot. Ancient hedgerows offer opportunities to spot wildlife and in the summer it's worth bringing a butterfly identifier, as well as some binoculars to get the best out of the views.

The Carpenters Arms

Located at the south end of the village, the Carpenters Arms has a crisp looking interior with a planed floor contrasting with the highly polished wooden ceiling. White painted walls add to the modern air. There are two bars, with one having a large screen TV, as well as a child-friendly garden. The menu has all the basics plus some surprises, including salmon in herb and champagne sauce, steak and Guinness pie and vegetable risotto. Telephone: 01525 240272.

THE WALK

From the pub car park, walk northwards up the main street, passing the village pump almost immediately. Look out for examples of different building styles as you go, including thatched, brick and half-timbered cottages. The road curves to the right and then left near the church, becoming **High Street North**. On reaching the **Swan**, turn left into **Chapel Square**.

The main manor here once belonged to Geoffrey Chaucer, an occasional visitor to the village, whilst St Michael and All Angels is said to have hidden Oliver Cromwell. Built in 1150, this is one of the finest Norman churches in the country, having remained largely unaltered since then. The village once had three brick kilns, which accounts for the predominance of this building material.

Pass the entrance to **Fishweir** and follow the concrete road to **Bury**

Farm. Pick up the footpath marked '**Circular Walk**' on the right opposite the bungalow, over a stile. Pass over a pair of stiles through a gap in the hedge and head half left over the following field, over another stile, and then half right, aiming for a metal kissing gate. This brings you out onto a pond, which you skirt to the left and then pass through a gate via another stile. Keep to the right hand edge of the next field until you reach a double stile on the right, passing through the hedge.

The path here follows the route of an old drovers' road where stock from Wales would be driven to the market at Banbury or even as far as London. In summer look out for the wildlife harboured by the hedge, including hedge brown and gatekeeper butterflies.

After the stile, the path swings to the left and is channelled through a hedge and fence. Pass through another double stile, turn right and cross yet another double stile. Keep your direction over the following field, aiming for a gap in the hedge,

Some of the delightful thatched cottages to be seen in

after which you head half right to the corner of the field where a stile brings you out onto a minor road. Turn left here and follow the road past the entrance to **Upper Dean Farm** and, shortly after, **Dean Farm**.

 ④

Keep with the road until it becomes a track and, on reaching a junction, pass over the stile ahead into a field with excellent views. Head half left to a fresh double stile in the top left-hand corner. Pass through and pick up a rough farm track, which soon follows the edge of **Blackland Covert**. Stay with this until you reach a gate.

Pass through this and to the left of the pylon towards another gate in the top left-hand corner.

 ⑤

Now follow a path parallel to the pylons, with a hedge on your right. Maintain your direction, pass through a gap in the hedge, cross another field and turn right onto a farm track. This brings you to **North Farm**. Enter the farmyard and follow the track to the left, following the left-hand edge of the next two fields.

The route here follows part of a Roman road connecting Dorchester on Thames with Alconbury, passing through Bedford. Archaeological digs have revealed evidence of Roman metalling beneath, so you are wandering in ancient footsteps!

Pass beneath the wires and over a plank bridge and stile within a hedge. On reaching the corner of the field do not follow the '**Circular** **Walk**' signs; instead pass through the rusting gate in front of you and head half right towards yet another pair of stiles halfway along the top of the field. After this, aim slightly more right over another stile and across two fields. In the top corner, the path heads left between two hedges and up onto a road. Turn left here and at the junction bear left towards the **Carpenters Arms**.

Place of Interest Nearby

Originally a Rothschild hunting box, **Ascott,** outside Wing, now belongs to the National Trust. Both the Jacobean house, with its collection of furniture and Chinese ceramics, and the gardens, including a sunken garden, are worth a visit. Opening times vary so it's best to phone for details in advance. Telephone: 01296 688242.

13 Quainton

The Walk: $4^1/_2$ miles
Terrain: Easy going and flat, with some boggy patches
Map: OS Landranger 165 or Explorers 192 (partial) and 181 GR 747201

How to get there
Quainton lies 2 miles north of Waddesdon, which is on the A41 between Aylesbury and Bicester. **Parking:** By the village green outside the pub.

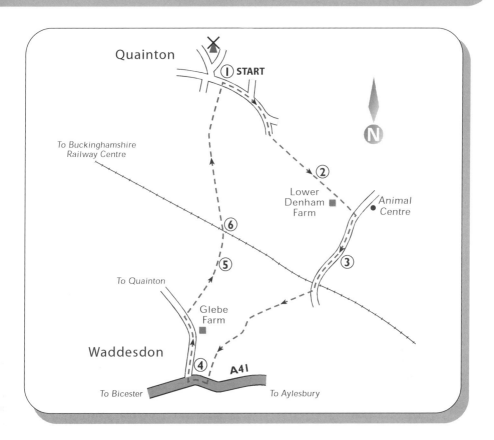

Introduction

This walk links the two Buckinghamshire villages of Quainton and Waddesdon, following tracks that have probably been trodden for centuries. The fields that divide them can get boggy so wear stout shoes, but there's always the compensation of constant sightings of Quainton's windmill on the way back. The route also twice crosses over the line belonging to the Buckinghamshire Railway Centre.

The route south includes part of the Aylesbury Ring walk, whilst the path heading back to Quainton is part of the North Buckinghamshire Way. These paths pass through working fields, so be prepared to meet with the odd cow chewing contentedly on the luscious grass produced hereabouts. The scenery is extensive and the surroundings quiet. Both Quainton and Waddesdon offer a range of watering holes.

The George & Dragon

This inn on Quainton's green, below the windmill, is a quintessential village pub. The walls are lined with banquettes, whilst solid wooden tables and no-nonsense chairs send out the message that this is a working pub. An impressive brick arch divides the bars and there is a section for children. A wide selection of food is offered, ranging from grills and steaks right through to vegetarian options. There's also a specials blackboard and a tempting selection of home-made sweets. At lunchtimes on Tuesdays the pub offers OAP specials with the possibility of apple crumble! Telephone: 01296 655436.

THE WALK

---

①

Head downhill with the windmill behind you and on reaching **The Strand** turn left. Follow the road down, passing a turning to the left, and pick up the public bridleway to the right just before a house. Stick with the bridleway as it passes through various gates, maintaining a south-easterly direction.

Quainton's windmill was built in 1830 from local bricks and is open from 10 am to 1 pm every Sunday. It is the county's tallest windmill, which it needs to be as it stands in the lee of the impressive Quainton Hill. Look out also for the preaching cross on the green.

 ②

On reaching an open area with a slatted wooden fence follow this to the right and then left and down a broad path. This passes into another field and eventually past **Lower Denham Farm**. Keep to the left of the driveway and emerge onto a road. Turn right here.

Blackberry Farm Animal Centre, 100 yards to the left, is an RSPCA animal rescue centre. It is open to visitors from 10 am to 4 pm on Tuesday to Sunday.

 ③

Stay on the road past the point where the **Aylesbury Ring** merges from the left and continue as it bends and passes over the railway, just after which the route diverts to the right. The path cuts across a field, through a hedge and over the corner of another field, then picks up a farm track. Follow this down for a while and rejoin the path on the left just before some trees. Keep to the right, with the path passing over a stile into the adjacent field before resuming its previous direction. After a while, head slightly right to pick up a pair of stiles. Cross these and head straight ahead, over another field and onto an alley behind the back of some houses, emerging onto the A41 where you turn right into **Waddesdon**.

Waddesdon itself is overshadowed by its manor, which is worth a visit (see below), but the Five Arrows pub and restaurant stands out with its half-timbered façade and multitude of Tudor-style chimneys.

 ④

After 100 yards turn right up **Quainton Road**, where the windmill soon reappears in the distance. Pass **Glebe Farm** on your right and immediately after a road sign the footpath passes through a hedge and a pair of stiles, also to your right. Cross a farm track and maintain your direction over another field.

 ⑤

On reaching the top left corner, turn left into another field and pick up the **North Buckinghamshire Way**. Stick to the left and, on reaching a corner, cut through a gap in the hedge and proceed over a stile and a small bridge to cross the railway

line again. Take heed of the sign and cross carefully, passing over a pair of stiles on the other side.

The Buckinghamshire Railway Centre, just up the line to the left, is an award-winning attraction with full size steam engines and an interesting visitor centre. It's just possible that you'll see some of the rolling stock in the shunting yards to the right of the track at this crossing point. Trains are in steam every Sunday and bank holiday between March and October.

 ⑥

Cut across the next field, picking up another stile to the left of a watering hole. Stick to the left-hand edge of the following field, aiming for the windmill. After a wooden kissing gate, stick to the right-hand edge of the following field. In the top corner, pass through another kissing gate into another field where you pick up your previous direction. The path continues as a gravel alleyway behind some houses, crossing a road on the way. On reaching the main road through the village, turn left and head back to your starting point.

Place of Interest Nearby

Waddesdon Manor, just to the south of Waddesdon, was built by Baron Ferdinand de Rothschild in the late 19th century to display his art collection. The house also has one of the finest Victorian gardens in Britain, and is immaculately maintained today by a combination of National Trust zeal and Rothschild money. Telephone: 01296 653211.

14 Ivinghoe and Pitstone Windmill

The dramatic landscape of Incombe Hole, passed

The Walk: 4¹/₂ miles
Terrain: Mostly solid paths across open grassland with steady gradients throughout, plus one or two steep climbs
Map: OS Landranger 165 or Explorer 181 GR 947158

How to get there
Ivinghoe is on the B488 between Tring and Linslade. **Parking:** The windmill has its own small car park on the south side of Ivinghoe, just south of the junction with the B489.

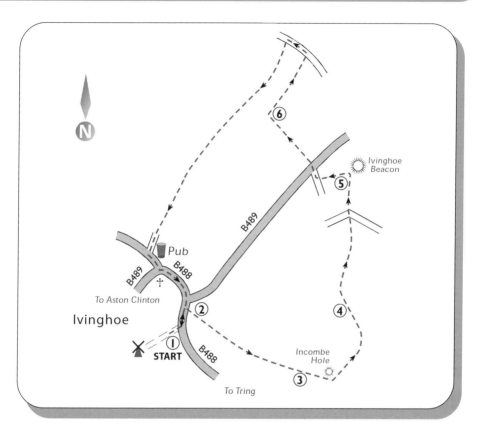

Introduction

Incorporating elements of the Ridgeway National Trail, one of our most ancient roads, as well as the Two Ridges Link, this walk starts with an opportunity to view one of the country's oldest windmills and leads up through dramatic chalk scenery to peak, quite literally, on top of Ivinghoe Beacon. Although it looks a challenging climb, the Ridgeway provides a relatively gentle path to the top, with the occasional climb along the way. From the top it's possible to look out across the Aylesbury Vale and beyond, with a commanding view that takes in the Marsworth reservoirs, the Rothschild mansion of Mentmore Towers and the Whipsnade White Lion carved onto the side of the Dunstable Downs to the north-east.

The walk ends with a long straight passage through woodland and ends up in the historical village of Ivinghoe, where it's worth a short detour into the centre to read the information board and maybe admire some of the fine Tudor architecture.

Drive and Stroll

The Rose and Crown

Situated towards the end of the walk, this pub is a good old fashioned local, popular with walkers. It has wood panelled walls, a cosy fire on cold days and an intimate bar serving real ales. Food is served both lunchtimes and evenings either in the public bar or the more relaxed lounge on an upper level, as well as in the garden in summer. The varied menu includes dishes such as escalope of chicken wrapped in Parma ham, loin of lamb or roasted Mediterranean vegetables. Telephone: 01296 668472.

THE WALK

①

From the car park follow the clear track up to the windmill and take in the first of a number of spectacular views, while admiring the mill itself. Return back to the car park, and turn left at the road, keeping to the verge and crossing over on the bend.

The windmill is a traditional post mill, that is to say, it is turned to face the wind using a large pole, at the end of which is a large wooden cartwheel. Look for the date of 1627 carved onto the base of the mill.

②

Pick up the footpath on the right signposted to the **Beacon** just after the cottage. This is an established path that follows an aged hedgerow. Stick with the path as it climbs steadily uphill. When the hedge runs out, keep going straight ahead, where you will see the route that will shortly take you up the hill. On reaching a stile, pause for a moment to look behind you for another of the promised views.

③

Cross the stile and follow the well-defined path. Below you lies **Incombe Hole**, which cuts its way into the landscape and it's easy to see why ancient man regarded this as a special site. Before too long, the path joins the **Ridgeway** path. Bear left, following another sign pointing you towards the **Beacon**, sticking with the wide path. Look out here for wild muntjac deer.

④

Go to the left of a gate and pass briefly through some woodland, on the other side of which the path descends slightly. Soon you will reach a kissing gate and another sign for the **Ridgeway**, which pulls you to the right and uphill again before heading down to a road. Cross this and take the path slightly to the left. One final dip and ascent brings you to the summit.

An ancient beacon that used to send a chain of signals across the country, Ivinghoe is also the site of an Iron Age hillfort as well as a very prominent marker for one end of the Ridgeway, the other being Avebury in Wiltshire.

Recover your previous direction and head sharply downhill. You need to head left, aiming for the road you crossed earlier, via an open area of grassland. On reaching the road, turn right and at the T-junction cross over. Pick up the path immediately on your left onto the **Two Ridges Link**. Continue straight ahead and slightly downhill, keeping the field boundary to your left.

Shortly after a telegraph pole, divert to the right across the field. Pass through the kissing gate in the corner and alongside the right-hand edge of the next field to another gate, which brings you out onto a road. Turn down the track immediately to your left, leaving the **Two Ridges Link**, and divert right where it forks down to a farm. A bridleway, this continues for about a mile through woods and comes out onto a residential road. Turn left at the T-junction. The **Rose and Crown** is on the left-hand side of the road after this T-junction. Follow the road down through the village and left again at another T-junction opposite the church. Stick with the pavement and cross the end of the A489 until you come back to where you started.

Unusually for such a small village, Ivinghoe has its own town hall. This hosted a Saturday market until around 1900, selling mainly straw plait goods from the ground floor of the building. St Mary's church has 15th-century bench ends, one of which is carved in the shape of a mermaid carrying a looking glass.

Places of Interest Nearby

Ford End Watermill, just north of Ivinghoe, is a restored small farm mill typical of the 18th century, with the unusual feature of a sheepwash in the tailrace, washing making it easier to shear the sheep. It is open on Sundays and bank holidays during the summer. Telephone: 01582 600391. Nearby **Pitstone Green Museum** follows similar times and is worth visiting for its collection of rural artefacts. Telephone: 01582 605464.

15 | Dinton

The River Thame at Eythrope

The Walk: 5½ miles
Terrain: Mainly flat, with some steady gradients and occasional boggy ground
Map: OS Landranger 165 or Explorer 181 GR 763108

How to get there
Dinton lies just south of the A418, about 3 miles south-west of Aylesbury heading towards Thame. **Parking:** On side roads near the Seven Stars pub.

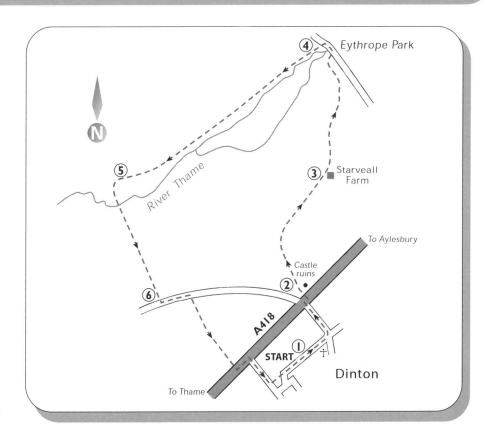

Introduction

This relatively easy circuit combines glimpses into the medieval and more modern history of the area, with a gentle stroll along a section of the languid River Thame. A magnet for wildlife, the Thame winds gently through open pastures, lined with pollarded willows, and at one point on the walk is dammed, resulting in a lake for nearby Eythrope Park.

This is a good walk for a picnic, with the river providing the perfect spot for pausing and listening to the birds on a lazy summer's afternoon. Amateur archaeologists will also have a treat, as there is an abandoned house complete with moat and its own fishponds towards the end. Dinton itself is a charming village with its own folly and Manor House, including remnants of the moat that once surrounded the latter.

Drive and Stroll

The Seven Stars

This pub in Stars Lane, Dinton, dates back to 1640 and its front section is made out of a clay and straw material known as witchert, unique to this area. Look out for the ancient, highly-polished settles in front of a large stone inglenook fireplace in the lounge bar. The menu offers dishes such as beef in beer and freshly battered rock salmon, with the dessert list also tempting, especially the fresh fruit crumbles and lemon meringue roulade. Telephone: 01296 748241.

THE WALK

Starting at the **Seven Stars**, turn left down a side road to reach a junction where you bear left and then left again, sticking with the main road through the village. Follow this round to the right and you soon pass **Dinton Hall**, a large, impressive manor house with zig-zag coloured roof tiles and stacked brick chimneys. At the church take the road to the left and follow this to the A418. Turn right at the T-junction and after about 50 yards cross over, where you will be see the ruins of **Dinton Castle**.

Never actually a castle, what is now a ruin was built in 1769 by Sir John Van Hatten as an eyecatcher and a place to keep his fossil collection – not inside, but imbedded into the fabric of the walls. The 'castle' is said to be haunted by Simon Mayne, the 'Dinton Hermit', one-time secretary to Oliver Cromwell. These days fresh candle wax betrays its use for ritual ceremonies,

although the structure is unsound and should not be approached.

The footpath passes to the left of the ruin along the edge of a field. Halfway down, the path diverts to the right over a stile through a gap in the hedge. Pass through and head half left, cutting the corner off the pasture, which can get quite boggy. Pass over a plank bridge in the corner of the pasture and bear right. Cross over another plank bridge in the corner of this field and head half left towards the corner of the next field, where you head to your right towards the curiously named **Starveall Farm**.

Just before the farm, the path diverts left and skirts some buildings before heading back towards the river. Go through a gap in the hedge and pass through the middle of a field. On reaching a gate, pass through and bear right. Now head towards a stile just up from the first of two stone bridges. This emerges

The folly known as Dinton Castle was built in 1769

onto a minor road where you turn left and join the **Thame**.

Eythrope Park to the right is the setting for one of the five great houses built by the Rothschild family in the Vale of Aylesbury and was constructed in 1883 to surround the grounds of The Pavilion, home to Alice de Rothschild. The watercourse was dammed in 1880 to create the lake.

 ④

Bear left at the lodge and take the path on the left at the elbow in the road, picking up signs for the **Thame Valley Walk**. The path from here is well signposted and broadly follows the course of the river, with occasional diversions to the right through hedges. Look out for the old moat at the base of a field.

Pollarded willows and black poplars are a feature along here and house a variety of wildlife, including hole nesting birds, insects and animals. Look out also for fieldfares and redwings, as well as lapwings and plovers attracted by the abundance of reeds.

On reaching a fresh plantation, pass to the right and locate a small clearing and stile in front of you. Cross this and after 50 yards you reach a junction of paths where you turn left, following a line of willows and crossing a concrete bridge over the **Thame**.

The area to the left was once a medieval fishpond with internal divisions to create a separate breeding area.

Aim for the top right of the next field and pass along a farm track. Bear left at the top and follow this road round to the right.

At the T-junction, bear left and pick up the path on the other side of the road, opposite **Cowley Farm.** This strikes out across a field at the end of which the path is channelled through two wooden fences to the left and continues left at the top of a garden. On reaching a blue farm building, turn right and pass through a gate back onto the A418. Turn left and cross over, going down **New Road** to return to your car.

Place of Interest Nearby

The recently refurbished **County Museum** in the heart of Aylesbury provides not only excellent displays on the local history but also an art gallery and the Roald Dahl Children's Gallery in honour of the author, who hailed from these parts. Telephone: 01296 331441.

16 Great Kimble

Ellesborough Warren

The Walk: 4$\frac{1}{2}$ miles
Terrain: Occasional steep climbs and some steps, but otherwise established footpaths and bridleways
Map: OS Landranger 165 or Explorer 181 GR 825061

How to get there

Great Kimble lies 2 miles north of Princes Risborough on the A4010.
Parking: In the lay-by opposite the church.

Drive and Stroll

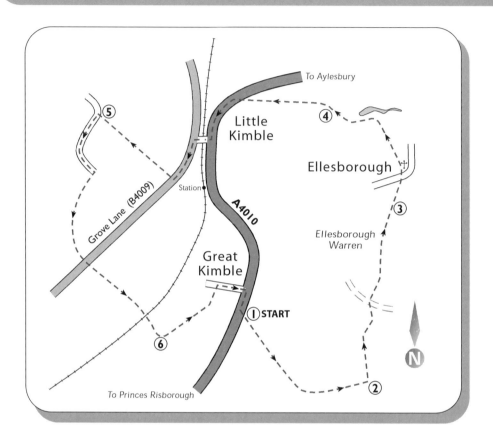

Introduction

This walk combines the chalk hillsides so typical of this area with the flatlands of the Vale of Aylesbury, taking in a number of historical sites along the way. Part of the route is through the countryside surrounding the Prime Ministerial retreat of Chequers, so don't be surprised to see men in dark glasses in the woods!

A feature of the first part of the walk is Ellesborough Warren, a curious geological feature of undulating ground and steep slopes negotiated via a series of steps cut into the hillside. This offers a good place to rest and even enjoy a snack, with spectacular views all around from the top of the appropriately named Beacon Hill. Later on, there's a lovely old mill pond teeming with wildlife and towards the end a fascinating field, where the remains of the medieval village of Great Kimble can still be seen.

The Bernard Arms

This pub sits on the side of the A4010 near the beginning (and end) of the walk. It is a homage to the Rat Pack crooners, whose songs dominate the sound system. The interior is light and unfussy, and is occasionally graced by a pianist. Tablecloths act as the main differentiator between the bar and restaurant areas, with each having their own menu. The former offers dishes such as salmon and cod fishcakes and chargrilled Caesar chicken salad or simple 'Rustique Rolls' if you only want a snack. Telephone: 01844 346172.

THE WALK

Pick up the bridleway marked to **Pulpit Hill Fort** on the left of the layby. This takes you up a fairly steep track through trees. On reaching a stile by a sign for the **Ridgeway**, turn left and walk alongside a metal fence across some open land to a crossroads of paths in the top corner.

The open land you pass through is part of a nature reserve managed by the Berks, Bucks and Oxon Naturalists' Trust where it's possible to see wildflowers typical of the local grassland such as rock roses and wild thyme.

Take the left-hand path and walk diagonally left across the field over open ground to another stile by a metal gate. Glance to the left for good views of **Great Kimble Warren**. Pass through trees over a small road, which leads to the back entrance of **Chequers**. The path then emerges onto open land. Keep to the path until you reach some steps cut into a dip, which leads you down into, and then up and around, **Ellesborough Warren**.

The Warren sits on the side of Beacon Hill, a small Bronze Age barrow, which was also used as a lookout for Napoleonic invasion and then as a gun emplacement in the Second World War.

Stick with the path across fields, negotiating a stile along the way and aim for the flint-faced **Ellesborough church**, sitting on its own mound. On reaching the road, cross over and pass up the left-hand side of the church. Cross over more open land and, when you come to a black hut with green window frames, bear left, aiming for woodland. Cross a stile and, after passing through some trees, turn right and on reaching a field bear right. This brings you alongside a small brook, which soon matures into a lake.

A view of the ministerial retreat of Chequers seen from

The springs round here are typical Chiltern features found at the foot of steep slopes where water that has passed through the chalk meets a clay barrier. The ponds are a reminder of Ellesborough Mill that existed here in the 18th century and which ground corn.

 ④

Just before reaching a metal gate, pick up the path on the left by a horse trough, which leads you along the side of some woodland via stiles. The path emerges onto a field where you bear right down to the A4010. Turn left. Cross over the road and stay with the pavement until you reach **Grove Lane** (B4009). Pass under the railway and continue with the lane until you come to a footpath on your right, which crosses the top of a garden and into open fields. Aim for the top left-hand corner and pass across two more fields.

 ⑤

On reaching the road, turn left and follow this round a corner, picking up the bridleway on your right shortly after a house called **Kynance**. On rejoining **Grove Lane** at the thatched **Clematis Cottage**, cross straight over and pass over a field. Go over the railway track, taking special care as this is a busy line, and follow the line of a small brook on your left.

At a junction of paths, pick up the one on your left, which then cuts half left across a horse paddock. Cross over a driveway and continue straight ahead, using the church in front of you as a landmark. This takes you past a small carp lake, with a duck house in its middle, and up to a road where you turn right via a stile. Continue up to the junction. The **Bernard Arms** is on your left and the layby is down the main road to the right.

The undulations in the field before the carp lake show clear evidence of the medieval settlement of Great Kimble, with platforms indicating where houses once stood.

Place of Interest Nearby

Whiteleaf Cross, 1 mile south of Great Kimble, is visible for miles around, although no one quite knows how old it is or what it's there for. Etched into the side of a chalk hill, the cross marks a site which has been seen as significant since pre-history and includes two Bronze Age barrows, along with one dating back to the late Neolithic period.

17 | Cholesbury

Part of the ditch surrounding Cholesbury Camp

The Walk: 4 miles
Terrain: Mainly flat through woodland although it can be slippery underfoot, so good footwear is advisable
Map: OS Landranger 165 or Explorer 181 GR 935070

How to get there

Cholesbury is on a minor road 2 miles north-west of Chesham and a similar distance south-west of Tring. **Parking:** By the cricket pavilion or on the edge of Cholesbury Common.

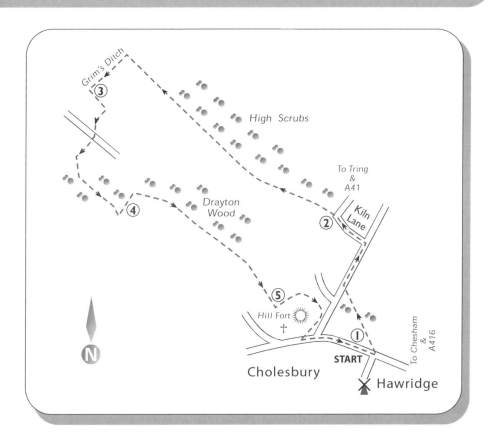

Introduction

Starting on the edge of one of three conjoining commons, this walk's main features are its beech woods. These are an absolute haven for bluebells in season but also act as host for wildlife all through the year. In addition, the surrounding fields are often home to show jumping horses.

There's a good smattering of history along the way, ranging from a remnant of the ancient Grim's Ditch through to the impressive sight of Cholesbury Camp, an Iron Age hillfort, the shape of which still defines the surrounding landscape today. Informative notice-boards give a lot of background to the site and allow the visitor to appreciate it in context. The walk also starts and ends by a windmill, now a private dwelling, which is clearly visible from the pub's garden.

Drive and Stroll

The Full Moon

Situated at the junction of Hawridge and Cholesbury Commons, this ancient hostelry claims to date back to 1693 and these days operates as both pub and restaurant. Inside it is airy, with an uneven flagstone floor, a variety of nooks and crannies, a low-beamed ceiling and, in winter, a real fire. Outside there's a garden and patio. Food ranges from sandwiches and soup through to delights such as a smoked fish platter or pan-fried calves liver with pancetta, as well as a vegetarian dish of the day. Telephone: 01494 758959.

THE WALK

Head up the road towards the **Full Moon**, with the cricket pitch to your left. On reaching a small obelisk, erected to commemorate Queen Victoria's Diamond Jubilee, head left across the top of the common and pick up the path between the trees, which strikes out half left and is marked as not suitable for horse riding. On reaching a road, turn right, passing **Purple Heather Farm**, and then left down **Kiln Road**.

Where the road bends sharply to the right, pick up the path straight in front of you, entering woodland known as **High Scrubs**. The path passes along the edge of these woods for a mile. Horses are allowed here, which means the path can get a little churned up, so be prepared for mud! Stick with the path as it emerges from the trees and, on reaching the last of three footpath junctions, turn left onto the **Chiltern Way**. This takes you down a narrow channel lined with trees known as **Grim's Ditch**.

Grim's Ditch is a network of ditches and banks that lies across Southern Britain, parts of which date back to the Iron Age. No one quite knows what it was built for although one theory is that it signified territorial boundaries. Appropriately enough, it marks the Bucks/Herts border at this point of the walk.

At the next junction bear left, passing across the top of the ditch. Follow the line of a hedge briefly and, on reaching its corner, take a diagonal path half right, cutting the corner off the field and entering more woods. Pass through these and, on reaching a road, cross over, where the path is corralled between two wooden fences via a series of stiles. After a brief interlude of open land, the path re-enters woodland. After 200 yards or so, head left when offered a choice of paths and left again at the next intersection, where you finally leave the **Chiltern**

Way and pass through a Wildlife Conservation Area.

  ④

On emerging onto a small track head left. After 100 yards pick up the path on the right that takes you into **Drayton Wood**. Follow along the edge of this until you reach a horse paddock, where you take a path on the right, heading over a stile and across the top of the field through a metal kissing gate and another stile. After a further brief patch of open land, you will come across another ditch, this time marking the edge of **Cholesbury Camp**.

Known locally as the Danish Camp, Cholesbury Camp was an Iron Age settlement fortified with a deep ditch. These days a ring of oval trees defines its huge scope (it encloses four hectares), that is probably best appreciated from the centre.

 ⑤

Turn left and follow the ditch round, although be careful as there are one or two steep dips and climbs. If you wish to avoid these, simply cut across the centre of the site, which is also a footpath. Stick with the marked path until it brings you out by the church, although the path passes across a stile on the left at the top of a barn. Cross over another stile and turn left back to your car, making sure to take in the windmill behind the pub before you go.

First recorded as a smock mill for the milling of flour, the windmill was rebuilt of stone in the 1880s and continued to grind corn until the outbreak of the First World War. In the Second World War it was used as a lookout post and it was restored from a ruin in 1968 and given a set of dummy sails.

Place of Interest Nearby

The Walter Rothschild Zoological Museum in Tring houses an excellent assortment of stuffed mammals, birds, reptiles and even insects. Bequeathed to the nation in 1937, the collection is now part of the Natural History Museum. Look out in particular for the dodo, whilst children always seem to enjoy the sharks. Telephone: 020 7942 6171.

18 West Wycombe

West Wycombe House viewed from the walk

The Walk: 3¹/₄ miles
Terrain: Some steep hills, with tracks that are fairly rutted in places
Map: OS Landranger 165 or Explorer 172 GR 825947

How to get there

West Wycombe sits on the A40 one mile west of High Wycombe. **Parking:**
In the garden centre car park.

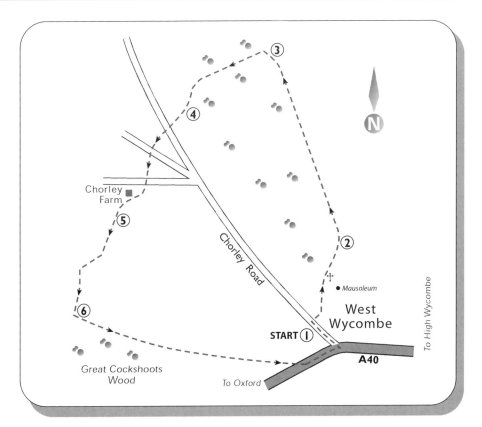

Introduction

Hanging onto the edge of Buckinghamshire, West Wycombe is a gem, with the village and house owned by the National Trust and an impressive church and mausoleum looking down on both. The walk starts at the garden centre, which also doubles up as a farm shop, where there is a large car park. The route is not for the faint hearted as it involves some steep gradients, the sharpest of them occurring at the beginning, but the climbs are rewarded with some spectacular views over the Wye valley and towards High Wycombe.

The paths are well defined and marked throughout and weave in and out of beech trees, planted here to supply raw material for the local furniture industry. To this day local commoners have the right to gather firewood from the woods. It might be a good idea to time this walk for just after lunch, with the pubs in the village a good option, but leave enough room for an afternoon tea at the garden centre café. Alternatively, if you plan to visit the caves, there is a café there also.

Drive and Stroll

The Garden Centre Café

This is situated in the Old Gardeners Cottage. The food served is wholesome and tasty, often using ingredients sourced from the adjacent farm shop. Soups, jacket potatoes and omelettes are all available, as is locally produced ice cream and afternoon tea. Telephone: 01494 438635.

THE WALK

Cross over the road out of the **garden centre** and pick up one of the paths heading straight up the hill towards the **mausoleum**. Having admired this, where generations of the Dashwood family are laid to rest, swing round the front of **St Lawrence's church** and emerge onto the car park.

The wall surrounding the garden centre lays claim to this being the oldest walled garden in the country. It was built in 1754 to supply food and plants for the house and village, with a fruit wall and grapehouse added later to introduce a touch of the exotic.

Head to the right and pick up a fingerpost sending you left on a well-worn track heading for **Saunderton**. After the effort of the hill, this stretch makes for easy walking along one of the ridges that define the valley, with beech woods either side of you.

West Wycombe Hill is a chalk downland, with mature beech and yew woodland. An Iron Age fort originally existed where the church now stands, with the current structure built in 1761 by the second baronet, Sir Francis Dashwood.

Stick doggedly to the path until you meet a clearly marked junction of paths where you turn left, delving deep into the woods near a depression that could either be a pond or, more likely, an old flint pit. White arrows on the trees mark the way. You now start heading downhill, gently at first but soon gathering pace, with a series of what are more clearly disused flint pits either side of you.

The path comes out onto the **Butler's Hangings Nature Reserve** via a wooden gate. Bear left here, although there is a wooden seat on the right should you want to rest and take in the view. The path's route is now clearly visible below you, wiggling through fields and across roads. The descent becomes

86

The impressive Dashwood mausoleum

quite dramatic for a while, with some steps cut into the steepest part. Cross over three roads, using stiles each time until you come to **Chorley Farm**. Bear to the left of the half-timbered farmhouse and up a track.

Butler's Hangings is an area of managed land known for its variety of butterflies and wildflowers. Cowslips, in particular, proliferate and you may also look out for a profusion of rabbits and signs of badgers along here and the following stretch, as well as the occasional roe deer.

  ⑤

If you thought your hill-climbing days were behind you on this walk you were wrong, as the path begins to ascend again, following a track. As you focus on the hill take advantage of the occasional gap in the hedge to admire the view to your left. At a junction in the paths near some open ground, take the left-hand option, which swings you round a bend and along the edge of a field. The hill now crests and when you reach the corner of the field keep going straight ahead down a narrow path between two hedges.

Drive and Stroll

⑥

More beech trees join from the left and, on reaching another junction, bear left, passing down the side of **Great Cockshoots Wood**, which is to your right. You are now heading steadily downhill and before too long **West Wycombe House** and the **golden ball** announce themselves once again and the path before you is well defined. When you come out onto a pavement, turn left and then left again by the **garden centre** to return to your starting point.

In 1751 the original 13th-century Norman tower of the church was considerably heightened and capped with a golden ball, which can seat six people. The view from the top of the tower is said to be the best in Buckinghamshire and the tower is often open to the public.

Place of Interest Nearby

West Wycombe Caves, dug into the heart of West Wycombe Hill, are better known as the Hellfire Caves, the venue of the controversial 18th-century Hellfire Club run by the then Sir Francis Dashwood. The caves are open to the public from March to October on weekdays and at weekends all year round. Telephone: 01494 533739.

19 Burnham Beeches

The Blackwood Arms on Littleworth Common

The Walk: 4½ miles
Terrain: Relatively flat, along mainly firm surfaces
Map: OS Landranger 175 or Explorer 172 GR 957851

How to get there

Lord Mayor's Drive, opposite the end of Beeches Road off the A355 in Farnham Common, is 3 miles south of junction 2 of the M40. **Parking:** On Lord Mayor's Drive.

Drive and Stroll

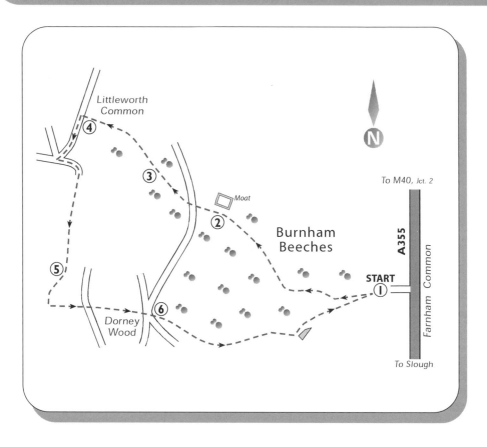

Introduction

This walk provides an opportunity to view what huge swathes of southern England would have looked like centuries ago. It survives because it was bought by the Corporation of London in 1879 to preserve an area of countryside to the west of London after it was identified as ideal development land. Its future is once again in doubt, however, as climate change is thought to be highly adverse to the growth of the beech trees that dominate the nature reserve and experiments have already begun with pollarding other species such as oak.

The walk takes you through managed woodland, with a number of helpful signs and easy tracks, although it is advisable to pick up one of the maps from the information points as it is easy to get lost amongst the trees. The route then heads out of the woods and into Littleworth Common, both to provide variety and a chance to sample the delights available from the local pub.

The Blackwood Arms

Hidden away in the heart of Littleworth Common is the Blackwood Arms, which despite its rustic exterior has a clean, modern feel inside, with white painted walls and gilt-framed mirrors. The excellent menu offers specialities such as horseshoe gammon, steak and kidney pudding, and even a 'Rambler's Fayre' special of soup and a ploughman's. Telephone: 01753 642169.

If you're looking for more basic sustenance, Burnham Beeches also has a number of **refreshment huts** offering sandwiches and tempting cakes at peak times.

THE WALK

Start by continuing west up the road where you parked, towards **Victory Cross**. On reaching a refreshment hut, bear right, passing through a smaller parking area and then a wooden gate onto **Halse Drive**. Although you are walking on a road here, this is in fact a car-free zone. Stay with the drive, heading first down a hill, to **Victoria Drive**, and then up again.

Look out for some of the ancient pollards along this stretch, with some over 450 years old. They were cut back to 9 ft off the ground to provide firewood – high enough to prevent local wildlife eating the fresh new shoots. Also see if you can spot occasional, apparently random, piles of logs that have been put there to provide habitats for small mammals, fungi, amphibians and invertebrates.

On reaching a crossroads, take the chance to divert right to take in the remains of **Hartley Court Moat**, which dates back to the 12th century. On returning to the path, take the fork to the right (not **Morton Drive**) down a less well made track, where there is an open space created by rhododendron clearance.

Although its flowers are beautiful, the rhododendron hides a dark secret. A non-native plant, the dense shade it casts prevents other plants from growing. Its decomposing leaves also contain toxins that act as a growth inhibitor, and the plant is also known to be a host species for Phytopthora, the Sudden Oak Death, a fungus that does exactly what its name suggests.

Pass through another parking area and over a road, picking up a public footpath on the other side via a stile, heading half right along another small track through woodland. Oak is more common here, with ferns and brambles carpeting the floor. Continue straight on at the junction, with a permissive path to the right, until you come out into an open area by a kissing gate.

Drive and Stroll

The path passes between two horse pastures and then, via a stile, down the right-hand edge of another wood, aiming towards a white house. On reaching this, cross over a pair of stiles until you reach a road, with the **Blackwood Arms** on your right.

The route takes you left, past a handful of exclusive houses and, on reaching a crossroads, turn left, picking up the footpath on your right after 40 yards through a gap in the hedge. This heads left over an open area with some good views out over the **Thames Valley**. Pass through another gap and walk along the boundary of two cultivated fields, with a hedge to your left.

The path curves to the right and, at the end of the bend, pass through a gap in the hedge on your left to walk down the side of a third, smaller, field. On reaching a junction of paths, bear left, cutting across the middle of a field. When you come to a road, go over the stiles on either side and down the edge of a field bordering **Dorney Wood**.

Dorney Wood was the one-time retreat of the country's Lord Chancellors, but in more recent times has been used as the country retreat of the Deputy Prime Minister.

On reaching another road, turn right and re-enter **Burnham Beeches** through its west entrance. Follow the path through a clearing. Bear left at a second clearing and pick up a fresh path heading left. Pass over **Victoria Drive** and, on reaching a T-junction of paths, turn right, keeping a wooden fence to your right. To your left is **Mendelssohn's Slope**, so-called because the composer was said to gain inspiration here. On reaching a junction by three particularly old trees, turn right. Cross over **Lord Mayor's Drive** and down a track leading to a pond. Turn left before the causeway and follow the track up and to the right back to **Victory Cross** and thence to your car.

Place of Interest Nearby

Odds Farm Park, just south of the M40, is a rare breeds farm offering a variety of daily activities such as sheep shearing, milking demonstrations, feeding opportunities and the opportunity to sample a farmyard tea. Telephone: 01628 520188.

20 | Hambleden Lock

Hambleden Mill, now converted into flats

The Walk: 2¹/₂ miles
Terrain: Mainly firm, with pavements and solid surfaces in the middle sandwiched by some field and grassland walking
Map: OS Landranger 175 or Explorer 171 GR 785865

How to get there
Hambleden lies 1 mile north of the A4155 midway between Henley and Marlow. **Parking:** There's a large (free) public car park at the end of the village behind the pub.

Drive and Stroll

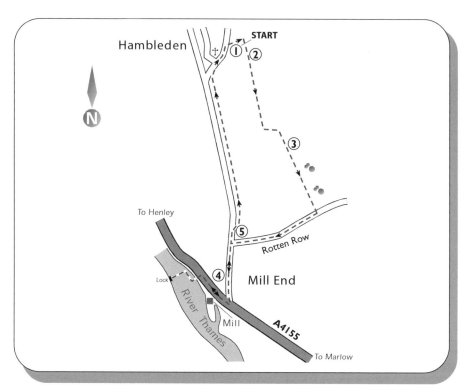

Introduction

Sitting in the valley carved by the tiny Hambleden Brook, the village of Hambleden may be familiar to many as the location for the TV series *The Vicar of Dibley*, amongst other programmes. The walk starts by taking you uphill sufficiently high to appreciate the views over the valley and across to the Thames, the circuit's mid-way destination.

The route has been designed to offer a mix of field and woodland walking, combined with river crossing on a suspended walkway and finally a stroll alongside the brook. The latter is a chalk stream, with the water that flows through it supplied by springs from the huge aquifer underneath and, as such, it comes and goes according to recent rainfall.

Both the weir and the lock offer a spectacular sight, with the weir acting like an elongated waterfall as it zig-zags a raised path over the river. The lock is significant as being the site of the first Oxford/Cambridge boat race, which ran from here to Henley Bridge before it transferred to London and these days is one of many operated by the Environment Agency along this stretch of the river.

The Stag and Huntsman

An oak-beamed local in the heart of Hambleden village, this is a 400-year-old, traditional brick and flint inn, with an intimate public bar facing the street and an unusual curved bar in the lounge. There's a good selection of food ranging from mixed grills that would challenge almost any appetite through to vegetarian (and other) curries. These can be enjoyed in the modern restaurant, in the garden, or in one of the nooks and crannies dotted around. Telephone: 01491 571227.

THE WALK

①

Turn right out of the car park and up the private road just past the **Manor House** on the left. The rather magnificent building is partially hidden by trees, but it's worth trying to catch a peek. Before reaching some more houses, the path offers an option to the right down a farm track, which you should take.

Continue on this track, parallel to the playing field below and, on reaching a bridlepath, turn left and head slightly further uphill into an open field, where you turn sharp right, following a hedge. Stick with this as the hedge runs out and the path reaches some woods. Go over a stile into the woods and then bear almost immediately right through a metal kissing gate.

Strike out across the field, following a line parallel to the woods (now on your left) until you reach some more trees and another kissing gate, which leads you onto a minor road sunk behind hedges, called **Rotten Row**. Turn right here and proceed downhill, watching out for any traffic. On reaching a T-junction, head left along the pavement. As you enter the small settlement of **Mill End**, cross over the road and turn right at the junction.

Hambleden Mill on the left was mentioned in the Domesday Book and was once one of 20,000 watermills in England. This one lasted longer than most, closing only in 1952 and today is a complex of exclusive flats.

After a few yards, you will see the entrance to **Hambleden Marina** on the other side of the road. Go down this road and pick up the footpath, which takes you to the right between two fences. This then emerges onto a series of bridges that zig-zag their way quite spectacularly across the **Thames**, following the line of the

Hambleden Lock

weir itself. Come in the summer and you may be lucky enough to see white-water canoeists taking advantage of the water. The bridges bring you to **Hambleden Lock**, an idyllic spot.

Having viewed the lock, retrace your steps as far as the minor road leading to **Rotten Row**.

 ⑤

Instead of heading up the road again, this time go through the

kissing gates and follow the path alongside the brook (which may or may not be in water), crossing straight over the bridlepath met earlier along the way, until you reach a small stone bridge. Turn right at the bridge and pass through the village, which has some stores where restorative chocolate and cakes can be bought. Head past the **Stag and Huntsman** back to the car park.

Place of Interest Nearby

Just 2 miles north of Hambleden is the **Chiltern Valley Winery**, which for over 20 years has been defying preconceptions about the quality of English wine. The cellar shop, which also sells beer brewed on the site, is open seven days a week and tours can be arranged if you book in advance. Telephone: 01491 638330.